The Cup and the Glory

Lessons on Suffering and the Glory of God

GREG HARRIS

Kress Christian
PUBLICATIONS

The Cup and the Glory: Lessons on Suffering and the Glory of God

© 2006 Greg Harris

Published by:
Kress Christian
PUBLICATIONS

P.O. Box 132228
The Woodlands, TX 77393
www.KressChristianPublications.com

Unless otherwise indicated, all Scripture quotations were taken from the NEW AMERICAN STANDARD BIBLE ®, Copyright © 1960, 1962, 1963, 1968, 1971, 1972, 1973, 1975, 1977 by the Lockman Foundation. Used by permission.

ISBN 0-9772262-1-2

Editing: Lauren Harris, Chris Doerfler, Traci Stephenson
Cover and text design: Layne Moore, Layne Moore Group

To my wife, Betsy

and to Cindy Walters

and to De Lee

—all partakers of the cup

and one day the Glory—

and to Roland

And James and John, the two sons of Zebedee, came up to Him, saying to Him, "Teacher, we want You to do for us whatever we ask of You."

And He said to them, "What do you want Me to do for you?"

And they said to Him, "Grant that we sit in Your glory, one on Your right, and one on Your left."

But Jesus said to them, "You do not know what you are asking for. Are you able to drink the cup that I drink?"

–Mark 10:35-38

CONTENTS

Chapter One

The Wilderness

In the chill of a predawn Monday morning, I walked down into our unfinished basement where I had a small office. As pastor of a church in Maryland, my responsibility was to write the monthly church newsletter, something I very much enjoyed doing. I needed to write to the church, and I needed to write to myself. It had been a life-changing week.

Berwyn Baptist Church Newsletter

March 29, 1993

"Place them both in my hands."
"But I don't want to."
Joe Hammond had just given me a piece of peppermint taffy, a ritual he had performed after every church service for as long I can remember. Ben, almost three years old, watched him as he gave it to me, as did my daughter Lauren. Being a father of two I knew the predicament of having one piece of candy that could not be shared. Doris Stough saw this too and graciously added another piece of peppermint candy she had in her purse. My children and I then headed back to my office. Placing my Bible and the candy on the desk in the foyer, I proceeded to deal with some office details in another room. When I came back to the foyer, Lauren had taken both pieces of candy.

"Place them both in my hands," I told her.
"But I don't want to, Daddy," she replied.

"Lauren, those are my two pieces of candy. They are not yours until I give them to you. I may give you one or both, or I may not, but they are mine to give or mine to keep."

"Place them both in my hands."

Lauren reluctantly placed both pieces of candy into my hand. I think she was expecting since she had given them to me, I would automatically give them back to her. In this case, I closed my hand over the candy and told her we would talk about this on the way home. As parents, Betsy and I do not want our children to take what has not been given them or to be presumptuous. We want gifts to be pleasant surprises and not perceived as some guaranteed right of their existence. We want our children to learn a gift is, well, a gift—something to be appreciated and never taken for granted. We also want them to learn the necessity of waiting; not everything that we want works out in the way we desire or even as quickly as we would like.

This vignette happened last Wednesday night, March 24, after our Wednesday night service. Little did I realize what I was trying to teach our children would in just a few hours be thrust on Betsy and myself as our heavenly Father would call for the same obedience from us. Having informed those at the Wednesday service of the serious problems in Betsy's pregnancy, problems discovered only on the previous day, and having been comforted by the love and support of these cherished friends, we moved in a dazed stupor as Betsy unexpectedly went into labor later that very night. As we rushed to the hospital about midnight, we knew the situation was quite grim for the identical twin girls she was carrying. As Lauren's earlier, my response was quite reluctant. Even at the hospital when we first received the news the babies yet to be born would not live, I still expected down deep inside if I gave the twins to God, then He would give them back to me. Until the nurses gently wrapped the first lifeless baby into blankets and carried her away from us, and then repeated the process with the second baby, I somehow believed there was still an outside hope for them. Only after the nurse walked down the hall with our second baby and turned the corner forever out of our sight this side of heaven, did I fully realize this was one of those times when God had closed His hand over what had been placed into it.

Actually, Betsy and I had not yet placed our twins in God's hands. It was something God did. We had no choice but to accept what He in His sovereign wisdom had chosen to do. Our part in placing the twins into His hands occurred for us after the fact when we acknowledged God is God, and God is good. If God saw best for the twins to be in their eternal home with Him, then we could—and actively would—entrust their keeping to their ultimate Father. This is the cornerstone of our hope and confidence in Christ Jesus.

Hours earlier I had instructed Lauren how deeply we loved her, and how we desired the best for her. I told her whether or not I gave her the candy she wanted was no indication of our love for her. These words were said probably more for my own benefit than for that of a four-year-old. Once more the Lord brought my own teaching back to me. God's love for His children is not only stated in Scripture but also ultimately demonstrated in the sacrificial death of His own Son, Jesus. Even more so, God knows firsthand what it was like to stand by and watch the death of His own child—and He could have intervened and stopped it at any moment. God has exhibited His love for us in not only making us His children, but in infinitely countless ways every day of our existence. His love for us—and for the twins—is not contingent on whether we bring the little girls into our home, or God brings them into His.

"Place them both into My hands."

"We have, Lord, and thank You for taking such good care of them."

> But we do not want you to be uninformed, brethren, about those who are asleep, that you may not grieve, as do the rest who have no hope. For if we believe that Jesus died and rose again, even so God will bring with Him those who have fallen asleep in Jesus. For this we say to you by the word of the Lord that we who are alive, and remain until the coming of the Lord, shall not precede those who have fallen asleep. For the Lord Himself will descend from heaven with a shout, with the voice of the archangel, and with the trumpet of God; and the dead in Christ shall rise first. Then we who are alive and remain shall be caught up together with them in the clouds to meet the Lord in the air, and thus, we shall always be with the Lord.
>
> Therefore, comfort one another with these words.
> —1 Thessalonians 4:13-18

May the Lord bless you all. We are greatly blessed and comforted by you.

Your brother in the Lord,

Greg

There. It was finished. Having a child or children die is something unnatural. I do not have anything with which I can compare it. I have found although you can enjoy life again, you never completely get over it. Part of your deepest heart will always contain a hole. I marvel how it is possible for someone to endure a child's death without leaning on the love of Jesus. People do it every day, but for the life of me I cannot bring myself to perceive how they do.

Nobody knows what to say when someone's child dies, and nobody knows what to say especially to the pastor when he is among the grieving. I wrote to the church to try to give the death of the twins the proper perspective, and as I mentioned, I wrote for myself as much as I did for them. I meant what I wrote then, and I stand by it today. Nothing has changed.

I had stepped into the ever-expanding society of mourners and sufferers. I had rarely been there before and never on this level. It is not a realm you enter voluntarily. Still in the midst of my overwhelming grief the underlying support and love of God were evident in a manner I never knew existed. Although the death of the twins was the greatest sorrow I had ever experienced, I could not break through the quarry rock of God's support of me. I existed in a composite of grief and grace, mourning and peace, heartache and hope—and I have never felt so infinitely loved by God as I did during this time.

I had weathered my trial, or stated more accurately, God had sustained me through it. I expected to continue with both life and ministry. A few months later I left the church in Maryland and moved my family to North Carolina. My brother had built us a house, mostly because the twins would have made us a family of six. We signed the contract for the house on a Monday; the twins died three days later on Thursday. We could not explain the timing, but we knew it was no practical joke with God. While pastoring the church I was also a professor at Washington Bible College. After the twins died I still taught at the college, commuting from North Carolina on Tuesday nights and returning home in time for supper on Friday.

An additional chapter was added almost two years later when I encountered sorrow's twin sister, suffering. Having just completed a two-week summer school session at the college, I returned home for the start of summer break bursting with plans and activities. My plans soon changed. I awoke the first morning I was home and literally fell on my face. Only with much effort could I walk at all. I had been involved in athletics all my life and figured maybe I had a small stress fracture from my run of the previous day. A red dot about the size of a large pea was the only symptom, appearing on the base of my right foot's big toe. My condition, however, rapidly worsened. Soon, my entire right foot massively swelled and had turned to a sickening blue-black hue. I spent almost a week in the hospital as multiple doctors performed countless tests and procedures attempting to identify what was so viciously attacking me. In the meantime, the mysterious assailant spread throughout my body: both feet, both ankles, my right knee, hips, my left wrist, some of my fingers, and even my jawbone. Massive swelling and excruciating pain intensified as the unknown marauder invaded each new body part. After a long process of elimination, the doctors determined I had rheumatoid arthritis, and had it quite severely. It would be more accurate to say not so much that I had rheumatoid arthritis, but rather "it had me."

I became virtually crippled for three months and on disability for seven. I eventually progressed to walking with a cane. Only after about a year could I attempt to wear shoes without getting nauseated. During the initial stages of arthritis, I learned a new definition of the depths of physical pain as my condition continually worsened for a while after I left the hospital. The arthritis became so bad that I could not lie in bed; my only "comfortable" position was in a recliner we had downstairs. Surprisingly the pain was not on a constant level, but would instead peak and recede. For some reason my most severe pain began about four o'clock in the morning. Throbbing would begin, intensify into frenzy, and then gradually level off about four hours later. During the throbbing, the sensation was similar to having my bones broken about every fifteen seconds, being so engulfed in pain I could not isolate what hurt—*I hurt*. Sometimes the prescription painkillers deadened the pain; sometimes they did not. I would break out into a full-body sweat, pass in and out of consciousness, not knowing whether I had previously passed out, and if so, for how long. I would grovel in the chair or on the floor, thankful my children were asleep upstairs and did not have to see me in this condition. They were six and five at the time. They knew Daddy was sick, but they were oblivious to the severity of the disease. After the throbbing ceased I spent the remainder of the day trying to walk on feet that felt as though each had several broken bones in them. At the early stages it took four to five hours to "loosen up." Night would soon come, and the warfare would begin all over again. This was my normal routine for months.

I began to wonder if I would ever walk or even stand up straight again. Yet, as strange as it seems, and at the time of this writing the arthritis has improved tremendously, I never was really all that much concerned about it. As with the death of the twins, I felt the reassuring peace and presence of the Lord. I knew He was fully aware of both me and my illness. I also knew my arthritis was abnormally severe in its onset, so I figured it must somehow be part of God's plan for my life. What I really wanted to do was preach again. I missed the treasure hunt of digging deeply into God's Word on a weekly basis, and the unspeakable joy of watching God use it first in my life and then in the lives of others. Not that one can bargain with God, but I told God if I had my choice whether to preach again or walk normally again, I would choose to preach. In simplest terms, I would rather preach while having arthritis than to walk normally and not preach. I do not write this as a bragging statement; it was merely the desire of my heart, and I believe God placed the desire there.

So I had a dose of both suffering and sorrow, but in my heart knew we had honored God. I fully expected Him to assign me my next ministry task. Since God had wonderfully blessed the previous ones I had been a part of, and since we had been tried by fire, I expected a substantially more extensive ministry.

Instead, exactly the opposite occurred. Far from having suffering and trials ending, they intensified as I unexpectedly stepped into the wilderness. The wilderness is a domain that I did not know existed. I was, however, learning. My first step in the learning process came when I listened to a Michael Card song entitled "In the Wilderness". His song perfectly expressed where I was. Before that I viewed the wilderness as a place in the Bible such as where Satan tempted Jesus. I also know now from additional studies that "In the Wilderness" is what many Hebrew scholars called the Book of Numbers, based on the fourth word of the Hebrew Bible. "In the Wilderness" is much more expressive a description than the rather bland designation of Numbers. I understand much more about the wilderness now than I did.

The wilderness is not a place as much as it is a condition. Nonetheless, it is quite real. Often we will seek to be with God away from the distractions and problems of our everyday life. We call this a retreat, or to some, communion with God. What makes the wilderness the wilderness is the *appearance* of the lack of God's presence. It is that baffling condition of going from spiritual light into spiritual darkness, and often you do not realize you are there until you are in its midst. I had been in a teaching and pastoring ministry for over ten years, and I know that nothing–*nothing*– can separate us from the love of God in Christ Jesus. While I understand and acknowledge that I am a sinner saved by grace and have many areas of my Christian life that fall short of God's desire, still I was actively seeking God and His work in my life. I was not a Jonah–I was a Paul. Yet, this juncture was unlike any I had previously encountered. For almost eight months it was though for some unknown reason to me, God did not desire fellowship with me any longer. I felt as though a close friend were mad at me and marked me off his list of close associates, without letting me know why, or what I had done to cause this. The wilderness is extremely painful, and it is extremely lonely. You do not have to be in a prison, in isolation, or under persecution. Family and friends can surround you in the comfort of your own home, and you still remain in the wilderness. In some ways, this was more painful than the death of the twins or the ravages of arthritis. I was more confused than I had been at any time since I began following Christ. I could not explain to others what I was experiencing because I could not adequately explain it to myself. I had reached an insurmountable wall. I had nowhere to go, and no way out, completely devoid of any direction or light. And by all means the hardest part of all–no apparent fellowship with God.

My prayer life changed considerably during this wilderness segment, being marked repeatedly by tears and anguish. Often I would speak intensely to the Lord–and for hours. In trying to explain to others what it was like, the best example I could think of was the Apostle Paul. In Colossians 2:1 Paul wrote of how great a "struggle" he had for those at Colossae and Laodicea. He used the Greek word *agon*, which is where we get our word "agony." What Paul referred to was his agonizing prayer for those at Laodicea. This one verse offers a glimpse into just how arduous true prayer can be. When was the last time you would describe your own prayer life as agonizing? If you want to be humbled further, when was the last time you would use the word "agony" to characterize your prayer life on behalf of others? If you want to feel totally unworthy, when was the last time you would describe your prayer life as agonizing on behalf of others whom you do not know? Paul had never met the Colossians or Laodiceans, yet he was consumed by agonizing prayer on their behalf. To top it off, Paul ministered his agonizing prayer while he himself was imprisoned in Rome. I have not consistently arrived at the last two levels of sacrificial prayer yet, but prayer for me became agonizing—and prolonged. I do not know what it was like for Jacob to wrestle with God, and there was no accompanying physical manifestation, but wrestling with God was what I perceived was occurring. Instead of God being the Paraclete or Helper, He seemed like the opponent. Instead of assisting and uplifting, He held me down and held me away—and I did not like or appreciate it at all.

Part of the pain during this time came from what others unwittingly said to me, but I knew God knew. As mentioned, my brother built us a wonderful house, partly with the twins in mind. Friends would compliment us on our house and comment on how blessed we were by God. Deep inside I boiled in turmoil. I didn't want the house—I wanted the twins. People who saw me crippled would see me months later walking or even running again and would praise God before me for His wonderful faithfulness to me in restoring my health. Again the dull ache of sadness permeated throughout me. I didn't want to walk; I wanted to preach—and I knew God knew. Similar to my arthritis scenario, this became my normal routine for months. I would pray for one thing, and God would give me exactly the opposite. God sustained us and met our physical needs, but not the secret desires and passions of the heart. Ministry opportunities vanished before my eyes. Students I had taught years before would excitedly call or write to inform me of their first pastorate, mission placement, or teaching ministry. They would inform me how great things were going, and then would thank me for making such a profound contribution in their lives. Although their situation delighted me, and it warmed me to have played some part in their spiritual growth, I failed to see why God no longer used me. It was not that I was better than they were; it was that God had used me before, but now He chose not to. I felt as though He had forgotten all about me. While former students actively worked in their new ministries, I sat on the sidelines and watched available positions for which I had applied turn me down. Frequently the human references I had were of such a magnitude it would be most unlikely I would not receive the invitation to minister there. Despite this, each ministry possibility would evaporate before me. I would return to agonizing prayer in the depth of the pit, wondering why God would not have mercy on me and rescue me from my despair.

Although I do not blame them for this, one of the hardest things to endure during the wilderness was attending different churches, especially those who deem themselves a "seeker sensitive church." "Praise songs"— which are misnamed because most of them are songs about us and what we intend to do for God ("We proclaim that the kingdom is here" . . . "I will go with Jesus" . . . "I will stand up for Him") instead of songs about who God is in essence and what He has done for us—were most difficult to endure. I would watch as the congregation enthusiastically sang about the Christian experience and how they would gladly take up their cross and follow Jesus. No sacrifice was too great—their victory assured—and how they would joyfully bask in the radiance of God's presence each day of their lives. I would be thinking, "You don't know what you're singing. You just don't know." I would hear messages admonishing people to accept Jesus. "He will give you His unspeakable joy. You will continually feel His love and His presence. You'll never feel alone again. Jesus will lead you and give you a sense of direction you currently lack. Life will have meaning and fullness and joy in it—all you have to do is give your life to Jesus and walk with Him." And I would be ripped on the inside. It was not what they said was wrong, it was only incomplete. *I was walking with Jesus,* but the elements of which they spoke were absent from my life—and I did not understand why. I thought how much better it would be to become a baby Christian all over again just to experience afresh God's grace and presence, but I did not understand why He would care less for those who had walked with Him for years.

I would return again and again to the lonely isolation of prayer. Repeatedly my prayer would be, "I do not understand. I do not understand." One of my greatest heartaches was as a father I have a deep and joyous relationship with my children. I also know Scripture teaches that God is our loving, heavenly Father as well. Yet, here was one of His children repeatedly calling out to Him in despair—but God would not answer. I told God, "Lord, I know you are a better Father than I am. Everything I do as a father, You are my role model: love, support, security, discipline, protection, and encouragement—I learned them all from You. But I do not have a parallel for what You are doing now. I cannot think of any situation where I would hold my children at arm's length and not want to be with them when they sought me. I will not curse you, and I will not deny You are my Lord and my God, but I do not like what You are doing. I would not treat my children the way You are treating me. I do not understand. I do not understand."

At the height of this intense struggle the college where I used to teach invited me to speak in chapel. Even the week before I was scheduled to preach I still had not the remotest idea what the message would be. Somehow 1 Peter 5:10 came to mind as a possibility: "After you have suffered for a little while, the God of all grace who called you to His eternal glory in Christ, will Himself perfect, confirm, strengthen, and establish you." Only a few weeks before, my family and I had survived a hurricane that did massive damage to our county and state. I knew the four words Peter used to describe what God would do were words of rebuilding and remaking, in some cases making something right after extreme devastation. I asked, "Lord, what can I tell these people? I believe You and Your Word, and know this is true, but I cannot speak experientially of this passage in my own life yet." It greatly bothered me because for the first time I was about to preach something I was not totally convinced would transpire— and I felt sickeningly hypocritical.

So battered, bruised, weary, and despondent, I hunkered down in God's Word. I did not set out to prepare a sermon or to write a book; I set out to find answers from God and His Word, trying to make some semblance of sense out of the last three-and-a-half years of my walk with Him. As with virtually everything from God, what I found was vastly beyond what I had expected or imagined. He more than answered my questions—He answered my heart. Then He patiently and lovingly bound up that which was hurting, as we would expect the Good Shepherd to do. What follows are some of the lessons He taught me from this, some of which I was most reluctant and slow to learn. They are not necessarily for everyone, but rather are intended for those who are presently struggling with suffering in some area in their life, especially the painful perplexity of why God would allow them to experience such depths of misery, when we know He could remedy it whenever He wanted. Hopefully, it will offer new insight into the graciousness of God as He lovingly uses suffering to draw us nearer to Him and to conform us closer to the image of Christ. At its heart, the lessons re-teach us the simple truth that God is God—and God is in control. We can never walk with God long enough to out-walk this essential doctrine; He will not permit us. If this book helps you or someone you know through their dark times of suffering, or even the darker times in the wilderness, then it will have been wonderfully worthwhile. I invite you to bring your heart and bring your hurt. But you need not bring your cup—God has one waiting for you.

Chapter Two

The Cup

From our initial prayer for salvation throughout the remainder of our Christian life, we continually ask God for something. Scripture both commands and commends us for doing so: pray without ceasing; in everything by prayer and supplication make your requests known unto the Lord; knock and it shall be opened unto you, seek and you shall find, ask and it shall be given to you. It does not displease God when His children make requests of Him; quite the contrary. What a joyous time of thanksgiving when God gives a couple a child in response to years of prayer, a directive light after so long a time darkness, physical healing for loved ones who are ill, or the salvation of a friend prayed for over an extended period. The list is endless. How bleak both our physical world and spiritual life would be if God did not answer prayer.

You will find, however, suffering changes the scope of your prayer life. It causes you to reexamine the content of what you ask, especially when contrasted with the pleasant junctures of your Christian walk. This does not mean you are wrong in asking God for things, but you will find suffering cultivates a different mentality regarding what you ask. Your prayers are not the same when you are looking up from the pit. In fact, an aspect of suffering occurs when God does not grant many of the requests we bring to Him, at least not answer them in a way we expect or even appreciate. Intense and prolonged suffering forces you to address in your own life the simple yet profound questions, "What do you want from Jesus? What do you want from God?" The questions are not as easy as they sound—and the answer is even more difficult. If you pray for a deeper walk with Jesus or deeper blessings in the spiritual realm—and really mean it—how God answers these prayers precious to Him may surprise you. It will most assuredly stretch your faith. Answered prayers of a deeper walk or deeper blessings are not so much a matter of God giving these to us as much as it is for Him to bring us to the point where we can receive them. The road to spiritual deepness with God is unexpectedly long and often severe with its numerous pitfalls and impediments. Once we grasp this concept, it will make us consider the cost before we ask God to have His own way with us.

Fortunately, we have such a request described in Scripture. In Mark 10:35-41, James and John approached Jesus and said: "Teacher, we want You to do for us whatever we ask of You." Before going any further, we might as well pencil our names in there next to James and John's. The content of our prayer requests gives overwhelming proof that quite often the desire of our heart is to have whatever we ask of God.

> *"Teacher, we want You to do for us whatever we ask."*
> *And He said to them, "What do you want Me to do for you?"*
> *"Grant [give] that we may sit in Your glory, one on Your right, and one on Your left"* [and we'll fight it out among ourselves to see who gets to ride shotgun and who comes in second].
> *But Jesus said to them, "You do not know what you are asking for. Are you able to drink the cup that I drink, or to be baptized with the baptism with which I am baptized?"*
> *And they said to Him, "We are able."'*
> *And Jesus said to them, "The cup I drink you shall drink; and you shall be baptized with the baptism with which I am baptized. But to sit on My right or on My left, this is not Mine to give; but it is for those for whom it has been prepared."*
> *And hearing this, the ten became indignant toward James and John.*

What James and John pray to Jesus—and it is a prayer, whether He was present on earth or in heaven—they ask Him to give, not to get God the Father to give. They also ask something beyond the present, worldly sphere, namely, to share in the awe-inspiring glory of Jesus. James and John receive much bad press concerning what they asked. Commentators describe them as selfish, ambitious, spiritually immature, yearning for worldly rewards, proud, and carnal-minded in what they ask Jesus to do for them—and again pencil in you and me there too. James and John had much to learn about what was required of them if they chose to follow Jesus. They had not at this point had their hearts torn away. But soon they would: at Gethsemane, fleeing in horror at Jesus' arrest, at Calvary, and during the appearances by Jesus after His resurrection.

While some of the accusations against James and John stick, there are other matters to consider:

At least they left everything to follow Jesus.

At least they valued the Pearl of Great Cost and pursued Him.

At least being with Jesus changed their priorities of what was of genuine value.

At least when many of His disciples no longer walked with Him (John 6:66), they still did.

At least they stayed the course and did not give up, despite their disappointments that the way God worked was often contrary to how they thought things should be.

At least they wanted to be in glory with Jesus.

At least they realized it was His glory, not theirs, and without Him there was no glory.

By the way, what do you pray for . . . when you pray?

At least they believed Jesus could answer their prayers.

At least their prayer had a spiritual element in it. They did not pray for worldly goods, riches, money, a mate, a job, health, a career, to have their business blessed, or a long list of other things on our wish list we call prayer.

At least they asked to be a vital part of the glory of Jesus after walking with Him for some three-and-one-half years. This was more than Judas believed—and vastly more than Judas wanted.

At least they believed in the identity and mission of Jesus and longed to be linked eternally with Him. This, too, was more than the scribes, Pharisees, and other religious leaders of that time believed or wanted. Instead of Jesus they desired places of prominence and authority so they would be revered by the masses, living a life of relative prosperity.

At least the prayers of James and John had an eternal consequence.

By the way, what do you pray for . . . when you pray? What comes after your own "Jesus, I want you to do for me whatever I ask of you?" How do you fill in the blank? While it is fitting and good God grants believers the privilege of prayer, we must continually evaluate what we desire of Jesus at the core level. When I look back over the bulk of my prayers in previous years, frequently I omitted eternal elements and desires. It was not what I prayed for was wrong; it was merely superficial, especially while simultaneously giving lip service to wanting a deeper walk with Jesus. Suffering was one means God used to bring me to examine the sum and substance of what I asked. What transpired was not so much that I purposely changed my prayers as much as the severity of the circumstances changed them for me.

So what James and John asked was not a repulsive request before Jesus, and was actually better than the elements of many of our prayers. But so much more exists in this account than we initially view on the surface. Our responsibility as good students of God and His Word is to step into the world of James and John "to see with their eyes and hear with their ears." Viewing this account from their world helps us gain a better understanding of what and why they asked Jesus what they did. After this, we will tie in what we learn with our own spiritual pilgrimage. Deep treasures lay embedded in God's Word, ready to be mined and assayed. The digging takes effort, but the benefits are life changing and eternal. And what we find may surprise us.

<hr />

The previous chapter before James and John's request, Mark 9, records the Transfiguration of Jesus. We tend to read about the Transfiguration rather casually, concluding it would have been nice to witness it, but it generally does not stir our souls. It did, however, stir the three who witnessed it. Jesus had revealed to His disciples, "Truly I say to you, there are some of those who are standing here who shall not taste death until they see the kingdom of God after it has come with power" (Mark 9:1). To a band of itinerant followers who had virtually no possessions, but who also looked to Jesus as the promised Messiah of Israel, this was a momentous disclosure, although they could not comprehend exactly what Jesus meant. By this time the disciples had already viewed Jesus' power over sickness, death, nature, Satan and his demons—virtually every aspect in His earthly creation. It would be difficult for the twelve to conceive of any other realm Jesus had not already subjugated by His power. But what Jesus now promised intensified their collective imagination, especially since Jesus associated this display of power with His coming kingdom.

As expected, the inner circle of Peter, James, and John were the ones Jesus selected to witness this anticipated event. The three spectators would come down from the mountain changed forever. For the rest of their lives, they would revert to what they had witnessed on that most memorable day. In fact, this preview of the coming kingdom glory of Jesus made more of an impact on Peter than when Peter walked on water, or any of the other miracles Jesus did. In 2 Peter 1:16-18, just weeks before his own crucifixion for the cause of Christ, in some of his final thoughts before his own death, Peter recalled the impact and importance of the Transfiguration:

> *"For we did not follow cleverly devised tales when we made known to you the power and coming of our Lord Jesus Christ, but we were eyewitnesses of His majesty. For when He received honor and glory from God the Father, such an utterance as this was made to Him by the Majestic Glory, 'This is My beloved Son with whom I am well-pleased'–and we ourselves heard this utterance made from heaven when we were with Him on the holy mountain."*

One usually writes or speaks about matters dearest to the heart whenever someone knows his death is imminent. Peter was no different. The Transfiguration was one of Peter's most memorable episodes in a life comprised of thousands of lessons and encounters with Jesus.

Also, the aged John wrote in John 1:14, "And the Word became flesh and dwelt among us, and we beheld His glory, glory as of the only begotten from the Father, full of grace and truth." John's declaration probably refers more than anything to the Transfiguration. Although Jesus gradually revealed His glory to His twelve (John 2:11), it was only in the smallest of displays. For the most part, except at the Transfiguration, the disciples beheld the humility of Jesus more than His glory. Even Jesus' resurrection and ascension did not match the display of glory God manifested at the Transfiguration. This may have been one of the reasons John recognized Jesus decades later when John was on Patmos; he had previously beheld His glory years earlier.

Nevertheless, the Transfiguration was a life-changing event for the three present. How could Peter, James, and John view the things of the earth the same once they had witnessed firsthand the glory of Jesus? Do you think having seen His glory, having seen Moses and Elijah, having heard the audible voice of God giving testimony concerning His beloved Son, they would return to the others the same? Would the longing of their hearts be to become Roman citizens and progress socially and economically during their brief and transitory lives on earth? Would they be envious for the sterile and burdensome position of a Pharisee? Do you think anything on earth or any position or rank that the world has to offer or any of its fleeting riches, would attract them?

We must remember Peter was also with James and John. He saw what they saw, heard what they heard. However, Jesus "gave them orders not to relate to anyone what they had seen, until the Son of Man should rise from the dead" (Mark 9:9). Notice the importance of Jesus' revelation: "And they (Peter, James, and John) seized upon that statement, discussing with one another what the rising from the dead might mean" (9:10). This statement is an important one, and we will come back to it momentarily.

When you read the account in Mark, it seems as though only a matter of days transpired between the Transfiguration of Mark 9 and the request by James and John in Mark 10. Actually almost a year went by. All the matters revealed in Luke 10-13 and John 7-10 took place after the Transfiguration but before the questions of Mark 10. This can be seen by the change in locale of where Jesus was with His disciples. The Transfiguration occurred on a mountain in Galilee in northern Israel. The events of Mark 10 take place on Jesus' final journey to Jerusalem—and occur only days before His crucifixion.

Still the Transfiguration never left the minds of the three witnesses. Although not disclosed again in Scripture, Peter, James and John must have repeatedly discussed the events and meaning of the Transfiguration among themselves, away from the other disciples—and likely when they were alone with Jesus. How much additional truth Jesus revealed to them—if anything—will have to wait until the full disclosure in heaven. But the Transfiguration glory did not immediately clarify much for Peter, James, and John; it only produced multiple and ever increasing questions—and much, much debate.

As with so many other instances, when Jesus did reveal additional truths, they often clouded the overall picture. Such is the case regarding the death—and glory—of Jesus. In Mark 9:31-32 Jesus again spoke openly to all the disciples about His death, concluding once more with the promise that He would rise again. The Twelve collectively—which included the three

Transfiguration witnesses—"did not understand this statement, and they were afraid to ask." Jesus' statements bewildered them—but their confusion was only beginning.

So after almost a year James and John did not simply blurt out their request to reign in glory with Jesus in Mark 10. What they asked was calculated and specific, most likely fitting for the situation at hand. Something must have occurred to trigger their approach to Jesus, hearing a word or viewing an event that moved them to action. A unique event had indeed happened—and when considered from the standpoint of James and John, they responded most logically.

Jesus had only a relatively short time to live when the events of Mark 10 occurred. Not only had He resolutely set His face to go to Jerusalem to finish His God-ordained mission (Luke 9:51), He also just as resolutely determined to teach the disciples on a daily and continual manner. Often the events of a particular day or an encounter with a group or individual would serve as the chalkboard for the Master's class on truth and life. The closer Jesus journeyed to His cross, the deeper the spiritual lessons He taught the Twelve.

One such encounter deeply affected those who witnessed it, namely, the account of the rich, young ruler (Mark 10:17-31). Not only did this lead to a discourse about heavenly rewards, it eventually led to James' and John's requests of Jesus. That a rich ruler would inquire of Jesus would most likely have caused the disciples to respond somewhat optimistically. It was not so much that they wanted someone else to join the Twelve. Rather, they would have viewed this interview as a positive event, a prelude to the changing tide of Jesus' popularity as they drew nearer to Jerusalem. Although Jesus had continually faced opposition from the religious leaders throughout His earthly ministry, now one came who not only had financial means and worldly influence, but who also possessed an interest in spiritual things. No doubt such a man would be a good catch for the kingdom. Unlike the majority who received the Gospel, this man had something to give. However, as often was the case, how Jesus responded to the rich, young ruler was exactly the opposite of what the disciples expected.

The man who approached Jesus lacked something—the recesses of his soul revealed this to him daily. Though he owned much property, he also concluded life must consist of more than what he was master over. He wanted and needed God, but he could not understand his current spiritual void. In fact, this very absence of God in his life surprised him because, by his own estimation, he had lived a righteous life, keeping the required law (Mark 10:20). He viewed himself as a good man, not a bad one. But his self-estimation was the primary obstacle toward receiving eternal life: his view, his estimation, his standard—not God's. Jesus, who searches even the crevices of man's thoughts and motives, addressed the man rather mildly by simply quoting a few of the Ten Commandments. Even these few commandments demonstrated the vaporous nature of the inquirer's spiritual base. The rich, young ruler came up lacking. He knew it—and Jesus knew it, knowing the depth of the man's failure sank far beyond these initial commandments.

Jesus quoted only the commandments that dealt with human relations, none of the first four commandments that instruct about man's relationship and responsibility to God. It was a fitting place to begin since here was someone accustomed to maneuvering in the material world and usually gaining an advantage. The man countered Jesus' quotes by insisting he had done all that God's Law commanded. Yet deep inside he knew he still did not possess the one thing that continually haunted him: eternal life. But his responses reveal that he defined eternal life by the parameters of his current status rather than by God's standard. Nowhere in his discourse with Jesus does the man even once refer to God. He wanted eternal life—but by his terms, his efforts. He wanted an eternal reward—not an eternal relationship. This man had acquired all he wanted—he simply desired to slow down the clock of life, or better still, make his current prosperity continue into the next life. But his internal emptiness contradicted his external evaluation. There still must be more to do, he reasoned to himself, admitting to Jesus he still lacked something (Matt. 19:20). Because of his claims, Jesus met the man on his own field of play, responding with a "to do" of His own: "Sell your possessions and give them to the poor, and you shall have treasure in heaven, and come, follow Me" (Matt. 19:21).

The question the rich, young ruler asked gives us further insight into his value system. The man asked what he was still lacking—the better question was Who was he still lacking. Mark 10:22 records his response after Jesus' invitation, "But when the young man heard this statement, he went away grieved; for he was one who owned much property." So by addressing the man in his own world—the world of the material; the realm where he considered himself blameless—Jesus exposed the fact that the rich, young ruler had, in reality, broken the first law: "Thou shall have no other gods before Me" (Ex. 20:3). The young ruler clung to his accumulated material gods that would never give him life or peace in its fullest. Instead they would only strangle him tighter and tighter the more he strove after bigger and better ones. The rich man came to Jesus lacking and burdened; he returned even more so, departing this time engulfed by grief as well. Grief is usually reserved for the death of someone you love dearly. In this case, it was the death of a dream, an evaporation of a self-defined concept of what eternal life entailed.

All the searcher actually heard from Jesus was the injunction to sell all he had—not the personal invitation to follow Him. The rich, young ruler could not comprehend the loss of the one or the gain of the Other. The grieving man departed that day without Jesus, without blessing, without peace, and at this point of his life, without God. From that day onward his massive property ownings never brought him any satisfaction, only a silent mocking that constantly echoed off his own depravity.

The disciples, however, would not have conducted this encounter the way Jesus had. Although they would not say it aloud, they were not fully convinced Jesus handled the interview properly. Their reaction reveals their thoughts. Mark 10:24 records that "the disciples were astonished at His words." Mark 10:26 adds, "they were even more astonished" when Jesus told them how hard it was for one who is wealthy to be saved. But why— why the disciples' extreme astonishment at what Jesus said? They had heard Jesus speak countless wonderful words and seen Him do innumerable miracles for over three years, and yet Scripture rarely records the amazement of the disciples, especially to this degree. What was it about this statement that would cause the Twelve to be so completely astounded?

The answer is, from the disciples' perspective, the rich young ruler was obviously already tremendously blessed by God. How the disciples reacted to Jesus' comments indicates how they viewed and defined blessings from God—and from our perspective as well. After all, is not the content of most of our prayers in essence requests we, too, may be a rich, young ruler? Rich in the sense of possessions we acquire, income, things we want, the financial freedom to be loosed from dependency on God. Young in the sense of good health, vitality, or as Jesus told Peter, "When you were younger, you used to gird yourself and walk wherever you wished." Ruler as one having the respect of others, prominence, a "someone," above the crowd, a well-paying position, security; we want others to look up to us—and we want others to serve us.

In essence, the gist of most of our prayers could be summarized as follows: freedom to do what we want financially, with the good health to enjoy life, while also being respected and envied by others—if not for what we do or who we are, at least for what we have. The content of most of our prayers give strong evidence we ourselves would trade places with the rich young ruler, desire the possessions he had, and still tack Jesus on at some point to our lives. It's how the disciples—and we—generally view blessings from God.

By the way, what do you pray for . . . when you pray?

As usual, it is Peter who asks the questions that most mirror our own hearts. In the parallel passage of Matthew 19:27-28, notice how Peter's mind works. By his way of thinking one could not be more blessed of God than the rich young ruler was. This man had virtually everything anyone could ever want, his cup overflowing with the good and bountiful blessings from God. However, Jesus told the rich young ruler to sell his possessions and "you shall have treasure in heaven." Jesus' answer surprises Peter. Maybe Peter better get this straight. So the treasure or blessing is in heaven only? Peter does not ask—nor at this point in his life does he really care—about the salvation of the rich young ruler, nor in why being rich is an obstacle to eternal reward. He wants to know about "us." And with Peter being Peter, if he were alone with Jesus, would in reality be asking, "What about me?" Peter begins his question with "behold" (Matt. 19:27), which is an extremely important introductory word. Its purpose is to point out the seriousness of the upcoming statement.

"Behold, we have left everything and followed You; what then will there be for us?" In other words, "We have already done what you asked the rich young ruler to do, but what he would not. We might not have had as many possessions to leave, but still we abandoned what we owned to follow You. What then will there be for us?" It's a logical question under the circumstances, and Jesus does not rebuke Peter for his interest in eternal rewards.

Jesus responded to Peter's question by saying, "Truly, ['Amen'] (in answer to the "behold" of Peter), I say to you that you who have followed Me, in the regeneration when the Son of Man will sit on [literally] the throne of His glory, you also shall sit upon twelve thrones, judging the twelve tribes of Israel." Remember, James and John were at the Transfiguration. With the exception of Peter, they knew so much better than everyone present what comprised Jesus' throne of glory—and their hearts must have leapt within them. Luke 19:11 states the disciples "supposed that the kingdom of God was going to appear immediately," and, of course, with the kingdom would come the kingdom glory they had once witnessed. Only this time the glory would not be limited to a fleeting glance by three confused disciples, hidden on an isolated mountain—the kingdom glory would shine forth unto the nation of Israel, and ultimately into all the world itself.

"We will be part of *that?*" James and John must have cut their eyes toward each other. It was one thing to see Jesus in His glory, glory rightfully due Him. But to be associated with it, share in it, to be intimately and eternally linked to it and to Him—what a reward! What a marvelous, indescribable, beyond-all-comparison reward.

Jesus then broadened His answer to embrace anyone (including you and me) who leaves people or possessions for the Gospel's sake. He promised an abundance of replacement, some while still on earth, but much more in the future (Matt. 19:29). However, Jesus ended His discourse in a curious way, "But many who are first will be last" (Mark 10:31). In Matthew's account Jesus continued with a parable of the landowner and his laborers and the reward that will follow (Matt. 20:1-15). He concluded the parable with the question, "Is it not lawful for me to do what I wish with what is my own?" And, of course, James and John are present, listening to the instructions of the Savior.

After this discourse, while continuing the final journey to Jerusalem, Jesus again took the twelve aside and began informing them about His approaching suffering, torture, and death (Mark 10:32-34). He once more concluded by promising the disciples He would rise again. With all Jesus taught His little flock in the past few days, this is a crucial concept. It is the same statement Jesus told Peter, James, and John immediately after the Transfiguration. This is what the three had been discussing, but also what they did not understand. Yet, whatever rising from the dead meant, it somehow tied in with Jesus sitting on the throne of His glory. Not only that, but it also connected the twelve to sitting on thrones judging the twelve tribes of Israel and receiving their long-awaited reward.

Jesus' statement about rising from the dead is the prompt for James and John; it is their catch phrase. Matthew 20:20, which records James and John's approach to Jesus, begins the account with the word "then," that is, the request by James and John comes because of the information just given by Jesus. This triggers the opportunity for James and John to ask what was already resident in their hearts.

Put yourself in James and John's place. They were witnesses of Jesus' glory at the Transfiguration. Were they not in a sense "first" to view the coming kingdom with its power and glory? Since Jesus said not to speak of the Transfiguration until He rose again, and since Jesus now spoke openly of rising again, even coupling it with the rewards to be given at that time, then the glory must soon follow. Also, since Jesus said many who are first will be last—many, but not all—James and John should see about securing their place. Not to ask Jesus might have been taken as an under-appreciation of what He offered. James and John knew their reward; their question is one of position. The truth is they beheld Jesus and His glory, and they did not want to be last in being a part of it. It meant enough to them to approach Jesus and make request concerning this.

Notice that James and John did not include Peter in their request before Jesus, even though Peter had witnessed what they witnessed. Mark 10:41 discloses the ten became indignant, and you can again pencil in they were led by Peter. No one would be more indignant than he; none of the other apostles had the same base of comparison. Peter probably placed a hard stare on James and John with the intent, "Jesus said not to say anything until after He rose from the dead. You aren't playing by the rules. You're cheating. Rebuke them, Jesus!" More true to his personality at the time, Peter was most likely mad he did not think of asking for this privilege himself.

What many people fail to see, however, is Jesus never rebuked James and John for what they asked. In a way, the request of James and John is a statement of faith and worship, even as a small child says things to his father that the father knows is from a child's perspective. ("You can have my dollar to get the car fixed, Daddy"). Jesus had taught them, "But seek first His kingdom and His righteousness; and all these things shall be added to you." He also taught them,

> *"Do not lay up for yourselves treasures upon the earth, where moth and rust destroy, and where thieves break in and steal. But lay up for yourselves treasure in heaven, where neither moth nor rust destroys, and where thieves do not break in or steal, for where your treasure is, there will your heart be also."*
> (Matt. 6:19-21)

James and John knew their treasure, they knew where their hearts were, and they wanted to be with Jesus forever.

By the way, what do you pray for . . . when you pray?

Jesus' response to James and John's request casts a piercing light on our own hearts and our own understanding, or stated better, our own misunderstanding of prayer. For instance, Jesus told James and John they did not "know" what they asked, using a Greek word meaning "to know intellectually; to understand." Scripture does not give any record of the facial expressions of James and John but they must have looked incredulous after the reply of Jesus. To them, it must have seemed at the time as though Jesus did not understand them. James and John "knew" what they wanted—and they knew He knew—and made request for it, being not at all ambiguous in what they asked. What they did not understand was the nature of prayer. They looked at their request as totally contingent on Jesus. He had what they wanted, He could open His "gift bag," wave His hand, and give it to them, much as He had done with the turning of water into wine and the feeding of the multitudes. What they failed to see at this point in their spiritual life was what they asked was not so much contingent on the ability of the One to give it as it was on their spiritual capacity to receive it. God is more than willing and gracious to give them—and us—what we pray for to the extent it accomplishes His own glory and our own ultimate good. The question is whether we are willing to let God bring us to the point where we are vessels fit to receive the deeper blessings from Him. So instead of "Give me this, Lord," our prayer should be "Lord, please work in my life and remove the obstacles that keep me from knowing You better and which keep Me from being the vessel prepared for a deeper walk, deeper service, and deeper blessings."

By the way, what do you pray for . . . when you pray?

Another lesson emerges from the previous point. Often our entire perspective of prayer is off-center from the beginning. We view prayer as

having to pry open God's hand to receive something "good" from Him—
something He often seems quite reluctant to give—when in reality the
delay may be with our own worthiness or fitness to receive. I cannot give
my six-year-old son a shotgun, car, or a chain saw. I cannot leave him alone
in certain places. Although he may think he very much wants all these
things, I would do him both disservice and harm to give him all he desires.
The parable of the Prodigal Son demonstrates the folly of having all we
wish given to us before we are ready. It is equally true in the spiritual world.
Do you not think Jesus desires deeper fellowship and intimacy with us, and
that He delights in giving good things to His children? Is the delay because
of Him, or because of us? In order for the Master to give James and John
what they requested, they would have to go through the grinding and
refining process of having Jesus increase and they decrease (John 3:30)—
and it will also be true for us as well.

Jesus taught James and John—and us—their whole perception of what
they asked was wrong. He did this orally, and the text itself does it subtly.
Six times in Mark 10:35 the Greek word *de* is used, which is usually
translated "but." This gives a new understanding to the heart of their
discourse. What James and John want is at variance with what they actually
were requesting, which they really did not "know."

Notice how the use of *de* ["but"] alters the tenor of the conversation:

> *"Teacher, we want You to do whatever we ask of You."*
> *But Jesus said, "What do you want Me to do for you?"*
> *But they said to Him, "Grant that we may sit in Your glory,*
> *one on Your right, and one on Your left."*
> *But Jesus said to them, "You do not know what you are asking*
> *for. Are you able to drink the cup that I drink, or to be baptized*
> *with the baptism with which I am baptized?"*
> *But they said to Him, "We are able."*
> *But Jesus said to them, "The cup I drink you shall drink, and*
> *you shall be baptized with the baptism with which I am baptized."*

Three times in succession the text indicates "But Jesus said" came in
response to what James and John said. It is though two different topics of
conversation were occurring simultaneously, and in reality, two were. Jesus
knew of what He spoke; James and John did not know, but thought they

did. The same is true for much of prayer throughout the history of the church, including many prayers we pray. Often we simply do not know what we are asking.

Many people, especially in a Christian gathering or class, will declare, "I want to know Jesus deeper!" If this is to occur, God must intervene to remove elements that hinder us from doing so. This includes even things we view as good and working in ways that leave us dumbfounded and confused. An aspect of this particular work of God is withholding or delaying temporal blessings so we can receive greater blessings in the future. Some blessings will be given while we are still here on earth; others we will ultimately receive in heaven, all carefully accomplished with the pinpoint precision of the generous God who delights in giving yet better gifts to His children.

"Why don't you give me what I ask, Lord?"

"Why don't you let Me?"

It is one thing to ask for deeper blessings. It is quite another thing to stand firmly during the refining process that makes us fit to receive what we ask.

"How bad do you want what you ask for, James and John?"

"How bad do you want it, Child of God?"

By the way, what do you pray for . . . when you pray?

We can learn another lesson from this one encounter with Jesus. In receiving the deeper blessings of God, we have a part and God has a part. Jesus asked James and John if they were "able," from the Greek word *dynamai*, which means "to be able," or "to have the power." It is where we get our English word "dynamite." Were they able to drink the cup He drinks or to be baptized with the baptism with which He was baptized? Jesus employed two metaphors in His questioning response, one active and one passive. In drinking the cup we do the action (active); we willfully partake of it. In being baptized we receive the action (passive); we submit to what God gives us. One is a voluntary choice on our part—which is by no means easy—and the other is to respond by faith to the cross we bear in whatever God brings or allows into our lives, to count the cost and keep going on in faith.

Are you able to drink the cup Jesus drank?

—The cup of not living by the world's standards of success.

—The cup of walking by faith (deeply walking by faith) even in the darkest dark.

—The cup of evaluating your own life by God's Word and His Holiness rather than your own perceived goodness.

—The cup of viewing the depth of your own sin and depravity and confessing to God and to others as needed.

—The cup of earnestly seeking Jesus above all else, including all attractions and all distractions.

—The cup of seeking first the kingdom in the midst of a world, including much of the religious one, which often seeks after the things this world has to offer. Left to ourselves the allurements of the world attract us as much as they do anyone else, but you will not find these in the cup offered by Jesus.

Are you able to discipline your life so that while everyone else may be seeking the world and its pleasures, you are seeking God? Are you able to walk alone with God, and, if so, for how long? Are you able to stand firmly against the multiple and painful darts from the Enemy who delights in turning you away from a deeper walk with Jesus? He has had centuries to perfect his barrages, and he is quite adept at what he does. Is Jesus worth it to get out of bed a few minutes earlier just so you can spend time with Him alone? Are you able to review your daily schedule and see that you have spent at least as much time alone with Him as you have in frivolous activities or hobbies? Are you able to turn off the T.V. so you can go to some isolated place to pray?

Although we will develop this throughout the remainder of this book, if you think drinking the cup is hard, it pales in significance with the baptism which God brings upon us because He allows us to experience suffering and sorrow we would never choose for ourselves. In fact, God sometimes allows suffering and sorrows so deep we would question His love for us if we did not have repeated promises in His Word of His unfathomable love—and even then darkness so overwhelming we still question Him.

How long are you able to walk with God through suffering, sorrow, repeatedly unanswered prayers, hopelessness, and spiritual darkness? How long can you walk with God—joyfully or just merely staggering along—when you cannot explain what God is doing in your life to someone else, because it makes absolutely no sense to you? How long can you walk with God while you have chronic and severe needs? You repeatedly witness Him answer the prayers of so many around you, but for some reason unknown to you, not yours. Will you still trust God? How long can you walk with God when it seems He has turned both His face and His blessing from you to someone else, and you do not know why? Perhaps stated in its simplest terms, how long can you wait on God until you give up on Him and put down the cup He offers?

James and John were not as spiritually strong as they thought—and neither are we. They underestimated both the extents of their spiritual resolve as well as the depths of the cup and of the baptism. If Jesus had shown them what comprised their cup and what comprised their baptism, they would not have waited until Gethsemane to flee in terror from Him. Nor would we.

We should also realize we do not "know" ("to understand") what we ask any more than James and John did. A refining process occurs that makes us fit to receive the deeper blessings of God. Yet our prayers focus mostly on the removal of the very elements God uses to bring us to the point of blessing. Is it any wonder why Paul would say, "We do not know ["understand"] how to pray as we should" in Romans 8:26? We pray for greatness and blessing from God, and then for relief from the divine procedure that accomplishes this. On top of that, we usually blame God for unanswered prayers, while all the time He is in the process of answering what we glibly bring before Him.

By the way, what do you pray for . . . when you pray?

Finally, it is human nature to turn away from the cup placed before us and not want to partake of it. Jesus had His own cup to drink—one whose depth extends beyond our finite understanding. His cup was so intense it led to drops of blood mingled with sweat as He wrestled in agonizing prayer with His Father. In contrast to the protective ignorance of James and John, Jesus knew what entailed the cup He must drink, and it repulsed Him to look even momentarily into it. Jesus referred to His cup when He was in Gethsemane, which interestingly means "place of crushing," where the olives were pulverized to produce oil that would bleed forth. We should wonder in amazement at the preview given in Isaiah 53:5, stating, "He was pierced through for our transgressions, He was crushed for our iniquities." Part of the crushing for Jesus began with His cup in Gethsemane. If Jesus had not drunk His cup, we would have no possibility of ever drinking ours. Even more to the point, our cup would have consisted of endless hell, eternally separated from God, with no Redeemer. When Peter attempted to rescue Jesus from His pending arrest, Jesus responded, "Put the sword into the sheath; the cup which the Father has given Me, shall I not drink it?" Jesus knew He had to drink it. He drank His because we could not. He drank His cup so we could drink ours. He drank His cup God placed before Him so we could become sharers with Him—forever.

During three sequences of prayer Jesus pleaded with God to have His cup removed from Him. He pleaded with a depth of agony greater than the combined agony of all prayers offered before or after the cross. But three times He also prayed, "yet not as I will, but as Thou will" (Matt. 26:39). That last phrase cost Him dearly—and it will you too, if you really mean it, and not merely repetitiously incorporate it into what we call prayer.

By the way, what do you pray for . . . when you pray?

Put your heart on the table. The Cup is our responsibility to take up and drink. Jesus offers it, but not everyone takes it. Are you able to drink the Cup He drank?

Please pass me the Cup, Lord. It's as necessary for me as it was for You. Give me strength and courage because what I ask is a fearful thing to me. Change me into a vessel fit for receiving not only what You would have for me, but also whom You would have me become. I have no strength to do this but by You. Strip me of me, and replace it with You. Have your own way with me. Thy will be done on earth—my earth, my life—as it is in heaven. Amen.

If you pray that prayer, you begin a new and different level of walking with Jesus, consisting both of astounding heights and astonishing depths. Walking with Jesus is a road to be traveled one step at a time, not an instantaneous process—and the road beckons us to come.

Chapter Three

The Road

The Christian walk is often a popular topic among believers. The phrase depicts multiple nuances of meaning: progression, continual movement, progress along a designated way. Since God wants us to follow Him—not lead Him, as most of us are prone to attempt—He therefore has a particular path He wants us to traverse. While much of the road we travel with God is beautiful and pleasant, sections of it are not. Some segments are surprisingly hard, steep, and desolate. We understand this to a degree intellectually. However, when we stay on the road with God—with God, not in disobedience away from Him—and still the walk becomes laborious, we expect God's immediate intervention. When difficulty progresses to suffering and suffering to sorrow, we question why God would lead us away from the light and into darkness. Then when the darkness increases, as conditions worsen and drag on, we have many questions we would like God to answer. However, it is during these deepest valleys that God so often appears to be the farthest removed from us.

Is it wrong for a child of God to question Him regarding the pitfalls and perils of life? As with many such questions, it all depends on one's attitude and approach to God. When you study God's Word you find God strongly agitated when people grumbled against Him, such as the Exodus generation in the wilderness. Not only did the people question God, they blamed Him for their harsh conditions, which actually were the consequences of their own disobedience. However, throughout Scripture you will repeatedly find another characteristic of people who walk closely with God, namely, that of fervently crying out to God for help, especially during times of intense suffering.

Two questions repeatedly arise from God's children in the midst of their trials: "When will you help me?" and "Why don't you help me?" The word that best summarizes these pleas from the heart is the word "perplexity." When—not if—you walk with the Lord there will be times when God demonstrates His power in your life. Examples of these include the deliverance from your personal predicaments, the privilege of seeing God use you in spite of yourself, and strongholds of opposition crumbled by God's mighty hand. However, there will also be times where it seems as though God, who has led you up to this point, quits working on your behalf; a time when God, who previously answered your prayers (and often quickly), now watches your helpless situation. He knows all about you—but He does not respond. You cry out to Him—repeatedly and fervently—but He does not rescue you. The resulting condition is one of perplexity. Grief throbs with the stabbing pain of suffering and sorrow; perplexity is the dull ache of frustration that never entirely leaves you once you walk in its midst.

If this is ever true of you, then you are in good company, biblically speaking. David, a man after God's own heart, learned firsthand this peculiar situation for those who follow God. Psalm 143 is an example of David's prayer for deliverance and guidance during an intensely perplexing time:

> *Hear my prayer, O Lord, give ear to my supplications! Answer me in Thy faithfulness, in Thy righteousness! And do not enter into judgment with Thy servant, for in Thy sight no man living is righteous. For the enemy has persecuted my soul; He has crushed my life to the ground; He has made me dwell in dark places, like those who have long been dead. Therefore my spirit is overwhelmed within me; my heart is appalled within me.*
>
> *I remember the days of old; I meditate on Thy doings; I muse on the work of Thy hands. I stretch out my hands to Thee; my soul longs for Thee, as a parched land.*
>
> *Answer me quickly, O Lord, my spirit fails; do not hide Thy face from me, lest I become like those who go down to the pit. Let me hear Thy lovingkindness in the morning; for I trust in Thee. Teach me the way in which I should walk; for to Thee I lift up my soul. Deliver me, O Lord, from my enemies; I take refuge in Thee.*
>
> *Teach me to do Thy will, for Thou art my God. Let Thy good Spirit lead me on level ground. For the sake of Thy name, O Lord, revive me. In Thy righteousness bring my soul out of trouble.*

Although circumstances differ, David's situation when he composed this psalm is similar to many of ours, as his supplications before God are similar to ours. He cried out for God's intervention and deliverance, praying that God would answer quickly. He looked back on his life, remembering the wonderful times with God in the past. At this point in his life, however, displays of God's presence and grace were mostly memories rather than the reality of his present situation. He pleaded with God as one who was sinking into darkness, as though death was approaching and engulfing him, and he would succumb unless God rescued him. It is a psalm of perplexity before God because God did not immediately answer when David called out to Him, but it is not a psalm of grumbling or defiance—and most assuredly not a psalm of abandoning God.

The Apostle Paul, so strong in the Lord and mighty in His Word, experienced the same spiritual condition. In 2 Corinthians 4:8 he described his walk with the Lord as one that caused him to be "perplexed but not despairing." "Perplexity" comes from the Greek word *aporeo*, which consists of *a*, the Greek equivalent of our "un" or "not," and *poros*, meaning "way" or "resource." Literally, the Greek word perplexity means, "no way out." Secular writings of the first century used the word to describe one hounded by creditors who was at his wit's end how to ever repay the debt he owed. Writers employed this word in describing a situation where one was totally unable to find a way out or solution, and for problems for which one had no resource for deliverance. The Latin equivalent for perplexity is "to entangle," which is a rather graphic description for the many puzzling items in our lives.

However, perplexity can lead to a worse condition. Perplexity expanded results in despair. In the Greek, there is a play on words. Despair is *exaporeo*, from the same root word as "perplexed" (*aporeo*), but in an intensified form that is difficult to carry over into English. If perplexity means, "no way out," then despair means "NO WAY OUT!" Despair is a much deeper pit than perplexity. Despair results not only when circumstances completely baffle us, but also when one is entirely devoid of hope. Paul wrote he was not at that point yet—but many of us have been, and many of us still are. If you are, you are far from the first believer to despair before God. Many personalities of the Bible, as well as throughout the long history of those who walk closely with God, have descended into the temporary hopelessness that accompanies despair. However, while despairing is common with many, it is not unavoidable. Since Paul wrote he had not yet been to the point of despair, maybe we can learn from him and apply his lessons to our own lives.

Paul had both witnessed the divine glory and been used by God to accomplish tremendous tasks by the time he wrote Second Corinthians. He had seen the resurrected Lord, founded many churches, and performed the great signs and wonders of an apostle. Even beyond these, in 2 Corinthians 12:1-6 Paul revealed that God even granted him a special preview of heaven. Wouldn't your spiritual life get a boost if God allowed you a 30-minute preview of heaven? Still, Paul wrote concerning his spiritual life and direction that on several occasions he was perplexed about what God was doing. Often, we think of the biblical characters as being on "automatic pilot" with God. Some Sunday School pictures show Paul as a robust and healthy man walking under blue skies, wind at his back, determined look in his eye, out to conquer the world for the sake of Jesus. I am sure such was true at times, but I'm also sure there were times of severe perplexity, especially since Paul said there were.

Consider for a moment: With all the spiritual privileges and experiences granted to Paul, why would he ever be perplexed? Paul does not answer this directly, but when we consider the events of one particular situation in Paul's life found in the Book of Acts, we might see the road he walked was no easier than our own.

Acts 16 records events related to Paul's second missionary journey. Paul was on a roll with God, a spiritual high. Evidences of God's blessing manifested themselves in virtually every aspect of his life. The previous chapter, Acts 15, describes the decision of the Jerusalem Council. The council settled the thorny issue how Jews and Gentiles should live together under one faith and in one church, the Body of Christ. Their ruling validated Paul's ministry to the Gentiles. Not that Paul needed additional validation for personal reasons, but if the Jerusalem Council ruled Gentiles must become Jews before being saved or live as Jews after salvation, his ministry would have been extremely more difficult. It was most assuredly a time of intense rejoicing and gladness before the Lord.

Things continued to go Paul's way. Acts 16 presents Paul in the midst of a ministry where he sees large visible results of his efforts. Along with these multiple blessings, the Lord added to Paul's bounty by bringing Timothy into his life, one whom Paul grew to love and to regard as his own son. Luke notes the importance of Timothy's arrival in Acts 16:1 by using the word "behold," which always heralds an important development or pronouncement. Timothy warranted a "behold," as he became one of the greatest blessings on a human level Paul ever received from God. Life simply could not get much better for the Apostle Paul as it was during this juncture.

However, after this list of multiple blessings from God, without warning and without reason given, the scenario of Paul's life changed. Luke shows this by using a *men–de* construction in the Greek text in Acts 16:5-8. Writers would use these words to show a comparison or contrast between certain items. The *men* could be translated "on the one hand," and the *de* as "but on the other hand." Notice how this affects the reading of Acts 16:5-8:

—16:5 *On the one hand the churches were being strengthened in the faith and were increasing in number daily* [success]

—16:6 *But on the other hand they passed through the regions of Phrygia and Galatia having been forbidden by the Holy Spirit to speak the word in Asia* [roadblock]

—16:7 *But on the other hand when they came to Mysia, they were trying to go into Bithynia (An imperfect tense is used in the Greek; they repeatedly tried to go; they made more than one attempt) and the Spirit of Jesus did not permit them* [roadblock]

—16:8 *But on the other hand and passing by Mysia, they came down to Troas* [never arriving where they originally intended]

Luke detailed the numerous visible blessings of God, and then introduced three successive perplexing roadblocks, disappointments, and occurrences that led to confusion—all for no apparent human reason. Of course, divine reasons were behind this, but God chose not to reveal them to Paul at this time. Since Paul wrote 2 Corinthians shortly after these events, and that is the passage where Paul noted his perplexity, this section in Acts 16 might have been the predominant one in his mind.

What we so often read over casually in Scripture would be a matter of intense conversation with others and prayer before God if we were the ones involved. For instance, the distance Paul traveled from Lystra in Acts 16:1 to Troas in 16:8 is roughly 500 miles, approximately the same distance from Washington, DC, to Atlanta, Georgia. Many of those miles were "mountain miles." Anyone who has ever backpacked in the mountains can tell you the difference between a normal mile and a mountain mile. Traveling must have been quite laborious and extremely slow, especially since Paul quite often was in poor health. Consider Paul's travel arrangements as he described them in 2 Corinthians 11:26-27:

> *"I have been on frequent journeys, in dangers from rivers, dangers from robbers, dangers from my countrymen, dangers from the Gentiles, dangers in the city, dangers in the wilderness, dangers on the sea, dangers among false brethren; I have been in labor and hardship, through many sleepless nights, in hunger and thirst, often without food, in cold and exposure."*

Any volunteers for the road to Troas? If you do, you are in for a long walk.

So Paul and his few companions walk, and they do not know where they are going. They walk, and every effort they attempt—even good and noble endeavors as part of the fulfillment of their call to the ministry—comes to an unexpected and unexplained halt. So they continue to walk, turning in the opposite direction from the one the Lord prohibited only to be stopped by Him time after time. So they walk, 500 miles from Lystra to Troas, not seeing the active hand of God's blessing in their lives. During the journey of Acts 16:5-10 there is no report of "success," no visible fruit, no churches planted, no lives changed by the Gospel, no seeing the powerful hand of the Lord operative as He had displayed just weeks previously. Probably as perplexing as anything, God disclosed no divine direction in the sense of where they should go or how long they should continue walking. It is one thing to have a ministry stopped so one can readily step into another. It is quite another to have one stop, especially one so fruitful, and not have another one in its place. Only at the end of this prolonged journey did God give Paul specific direction through a vision, and they crossed over into Macedonia to begin the first Christian ministry in Europe (Acts 16:10).

I immensely enjoyed the classes I taught at Washington Bible College, especially with the freshman. First-year students often have a frankness about them that we who have walked longer with the Lord often disguise by smoothing over and hiding our rough edges. Our roughness is still there; it is just not as readily visible to others. It would be appropriate, and even expected, to be stopped in the middle of the lesson and have one or more students ask, "That was Paul—but what about me? I haven't seen any visions. What do I do when I am perplexed? What do I do when it seems as though God divinely removes His hands from my life? What do I do when it seems as though the blessings and provisions of God are merely memories of my past?" Good questions, and of course, God provides even better answers.

While the particulars of Paul's situation are not the same as ours, we can nonetheless learn biblical principles appropriate for our own times of perplexity. While Luke described a genuine situation in the life of the Apostle Paul when Paul walked from Lystra to Troas, he also recorded a spiritual journey for Paul as well. The road to Troas was a walk by faith in the midst of spiritual darkness as much as it was a geographical journey from one point to another. But God does not reserve such perplexing journeys only for the Apostle Pauls of this world. We who desire to walk with Jesus must all travel that same spiritual road with the Lord. While some similarities between your road and someone else's may be evident, the particular path God leads you on is uniquely yours, containing different bends and twists, mountains and valleys. Your "road to Troas" may involve . . .

—Direction in your life where you actively seek God's will.

—Direction in your life concerning finances.

—Direction in your life concerning your mate for life, or whether God is going to give you a mate for life.

—Direction in your life concerning a present crisis where no one but God can sufficiently work.

—Direction in your life regarding anything else that continually perplexes you, any predicament in which you see "no way out," and your only viable option is to wait, perhaps even for a long time, for God's specific solution or direction.

Let's drop down into Paul's world and walk to Troas—not so much with Paul—but especially with Jesus. Let's look at the account in Scripture, and then honestly evaluate our lives before the Lord.

As a foundational place to begin, it must be noted that Paul was living in obedience to God when God twice told him "no" to what he attempted. Paul was not like Jonah; he was walking with God, not running away from Him. We begin at the same place before going any farther. The first element before crying out to God "Why?" or "Help!" is to examine your own life. Are you currently living in obedience to God? Most of us know whether we are obediently walking with the Lord or not. If there's any confusion—when really there should not be, the Holy Spirit by no means has lost His ability to convict of sin—simply ask God to show you if you are living in obedience to His will. But you had better mean business because God most assuredly does. As long as we live there will always be items in our lives God continually refines as He conforms us to the image of Christ. However, a stark division exists between being in the process of sanctification versus being in direct and rebellious disobedience before God—and most of us know the difference with very little searching.

Making sure we are in obedience to God involves a related feature that we often overlook. A vital aspect for the test for obedience is to see whether God is the center of every realm of your life (dating, finances, direction, etc.). Obedience to God, however, does not merely mean the avoidance of sin; it involves the active incorporation of God in all areas of our lives. For some people this may be more difficult to resolve than some active sin with which they struggle, but we have to establish this groundwork before moving on the road to Troas. The road before us is difficult enough without bringing along our extra baggage to slow us down and impede our progress.

A second foundational element is that Paul walked by faith. This sounds so childishly simple, but then again, we usually lose ground in our walk when we stop trusting God as a child would trust, erroneously assuming we have matured beyond that point. Paul continued on to Troas not knowing where he was going or how long it would take him to get there. If you are looking for God to reveal the outcome of His plans for you before His timing, you will be highly disappointed with God. Only after Paul had completed hundreds of miles and arrived at Troas could he conclude where God wanted him to go (Acts 16:10). While on the road to Troas, Paul had not the slightest indication of God's positive direction—and neither will we. The Bible describes this as walking by faith, not by sight. It is not at all easy, but you will not take many steps on the road without it.

How are you doing so far? Want to gauge your spiritual resolve by another test? Try this one: Paul did not stop walking with God even after God prohibited him from going where he first intended to go. What about you? The temptation to abandon Jesus after disappointment is nothing new. John 6 speaks of those interested in the Jesus who provided physical provisions (the chapter begins with the feeding of the 5,000), but not the Jesus who claims equality with God and calls us to forsake all else to follow Him. John 6:66 records a statement true for any generation or individual who follows Jesus: "As a result of this many of His disciples withdrew, and were not walking with Him any more." In the next verse Jesus asked the disciples the same question He also asks us, "You do not want to go away also, do you?" It's easy to walk with God when He exhibits the visible hand of His blessing. However, Jesus calls us actively and continually to walk with Him—even when we can sense neither His presence nor His blessing—and not merely when you see Him feed the 5,000. Many on the way soon leave at this point, determining in their heart that the road is too difficult to traverse, if it is passable at all. If you are to continue on your own road to Troas with the Lord, you must purpose in your heart you will continue with Him no matter what, and you need to purpose it before you go very far. If you fail to do so, the steepness of the ascents—and descents—will turn you back rather quickly.

A positive aspect in God's dealing with Paul is also evident in Acts 16. A "no" from God is just as much of a divine direction-indicator as was the positive revelation of the Macedonian vision. While a "no" from God will not tell you where, it will tell you where not. Contrary to what you may hear, there are actually some good and legitimate endeavors and even ministries God does not want you involved with, at least at this time, or perhaps never. So often we humanly view a "no" from God as a failure on our part. We tried this, but someone else was chosen. We wanted to go, but we could not gain entrance. If all the previously mentioned elements are in place, we need to realize that the "no" originates from God. God remains aware and actively involved in directing our lives. A certain liberation takes place when we appropriate this by faith. Instead of looking at "no" as a personal failure, we can view it as an aspect of the overall direct and particular plan God has for us. Instead of "no" highlighting deficiencies and limitations on our part, we can view it as the active work of our heavenly Father who masterminds the paths and timetable we are to travel, as well as the means necessary to bring us there. Such recognition is not an escapist mentality—rather it is the appraising of your circumstances through the grid of biblical truth. However, as before, the previous elements of obedience and faith must be operative. If you are truly walking with the Lord, a "no" really is from God. Luke emphasized this in the text by noting the active involvement of the Holy Spirit (16:6), Spirit of Jesus (16:7), and God the Father (16:10). It is no coincidence Luke presented all the members of the Trinity in a passage where humanly it appears that none were working. Walking by faith comes down to the proper spiritual perspective—and you must have it when you are on the road to Troas with the Lord. A "no" from God does not equal abandonment; it equals the process of divine direction, but the process may be a long one.

"But He still hasn't shown me where! Why does He wait so long?"

Well, for one thing the process is not complete. Before we blame God, we must administer a few more self-tests. Here is one of the hardest for some of us: The goal must be to follow Jesus Christ—not to go to Asia or Bithynia. Often, the case with so many of us (myself included), is we will pursue something, even something in and of itself good or noble. We can see potential fruit and how God, by His grace, can use us in that area. We come right up to the point of entering—and God stops us. If Paul had set his heart on entering Asia or Bithynia, instead of on following Christ, then he most likely would have become bitter, discouraged, and disillusioned with God. We will be too. Our goal, similarly, must not be:

—to get married—but to follow Jesus
—to go to a certain city or state—but to follow Jesus
—to do a desired activity or ministry—but to follow Jesus
—to be successful in whatever we do—but to follow Jesus
—to receive only good things in life—but to follow Jesus

God may very well bless us many times over in multiple areas of our lives, even above and beyond the elements of the previous list. Nor does this mean we should not pray regarding worldly matters and concerns. After all, God is the God who gives. He knows we have needs and concerns, and graciously provides for us. Yet it does mean "seek ye first the kingdom of God and His righteousness." You can have only one ultimate goal in life; all the others are merely correlated subsidiaries. Jesus did not restrict His command to seek God first to our initial reception of Him at salvation. It should be a progressing and maturing process—and an evident one—as we grow in our relationship with Him. We often do not seek first the kingdom of God as we should, but we can never leave this premise— God will so work in our lives to remind us if we do. What we must continually guard against is keeping one of the blessings of God from becoming the main goal, instead of God Himself. We can easily slide into that mindset without even realizing it, and it takes a concentrated effort to get the focus back where it belongs. This is actually no different from Jesus telling Peter, "You follow Me," after Peter wanted to know what would happen to John in the future. Jesus requires the same of us: you follow Him, not merely what He gives.

Finally, with all needed factors in place, you have God's Word; He will give you the direction you need. However, it will be in His time and by the means He chooses. You may not get a vision from Jesus as Paul did anymore than you will get a preview of heaven. However, we should not conclude God leads only through direct vision. Proverbs 3:5-6 teaches, "Trust in the Lord with all thine heart and lean not unto Thy own understanding; in all thy ways acknowledge Him, and He will direct thy paths." These verses simply form a synopsis of what we should do on our own road to Troas: Walk in obedience, walk by faith, continue to walk even after God says "no" to a good thing, recognize the importance of a "no" from God as part of the process of divine direction, evaluating and even redirecting our perspective, if necessary. But above all else, make sure your goal is to follow Jesus, wherever and whenever He leads.

<hr />

It is not easy walking on the road to Troas. You do not understand what God is doing in your own life. You do not understand how the personal blessings and visible fruit of Acts 16:5 turns into the wilderness journey of 16:6-8. When others ask you, "How are you doing?" or "What are you doing?," it sounds so ridiculously naive to say, "I don't know."

It's not fun walking to Troas, to be in a situation where it seems as though God's blessing is something in the past for you, as it appears He has turned His smile to someone else. When you're walking on the road to Troas, you cannot even give yourself away. Everything you try to do—even good endeavors with good motives—receives a divine prohibition. The only answer you get is, "Keep walking," and even that answer being derived only because you have no alternative other than to give up on God.

It can be quite lonely while walking to Troas. You will find fewer and fewer people with you the farther along you walk. Multiple exits of escape tempt and allure along the way, and many take advantage of this avenue of departure from the road to Troas. Still the road remains, and the Lord beckons us to follow.

Two related items the road to Troas will reveal to you: the degree you really trust God, and the degree that you are pliable in His hand. Do you trust God only when He gives you your heart's delight, or can you trust Him when He does not? You will learn all about this—and all about yourself—on the road to Troas.

It is a lot easier to watch someone else's journey on the road to Troas, such as the Apostle Paul's. However, God does not reserve the road only for the "super spiritual." Most of us want to see God do great things in our lives. Most of us, but not all, want to see God do great things through us, to make great impacts on people's lives for the Lord Jesus Christ, to be fruitful. Most of us desire a deep and intimate walk with God—to know Him and the power of His resurrection as a daily component in our lives. But will you walk the road to Troas—not alone, but alone with Jesus—so He can mold you, develop you, and accomplish His divine purpose? We should note we might never understand God's reasons for our unique walk with Him this side of heaven, which often makes the walk more burdensome. Yet sometimes He allows us to see His purpose. For instance, there never would have been a Philippian church, which turned out to be Paul's "joyful remembrance" church, unless God had said "no" before to what Paul attempted—and unless Paul had faithfully walked with God. With this there would have been no Book of Philippians to encourage and edify millions throughout the Church Age. Actually, I am very glad God told Paul "no," and I am learning to become glad when He does so with me.

Where are you now? Sometimes you cannot tell. The road to Troas may be around the corner for you. Are you ready to go? Some of you may already be in the midst of your own journey to Troas. You may only now realize you are on this road and actually have been for some time. The only thing is that you do not know whether you are at the first mile or close to the five hundredth. Such matters are merely subsidiary concerns to the primary one. Jesus asks you the same thing He asked His original followers, "You don't want to go away also, do you?" Do you? No one can make that decision for you. No one can walk your road to Troas but you—and the Lord still beckons us to follow Him.

A few years ago I received an invitation to perform a wedding on the Eastern Shore of Maryland. I asked my daughter Lauren, who was four-years-old at the time, if she wanted to go with me. It was her first wedding, and she responded with the refreshing enthusiasm of an excited child. The trip, however, took a little longer than her young mind imagined it would take. As she sat in the front of the car in her car seat, Lauren had only a limited view of the highway in front of her. About halfway through the trip, she began to question me.

"Where are we, Daddy?"

"We're right where we should be, Darling." (How do you explain mileage to a four-year-old?)

"But I can't see where we're going."

"But I can, and I can see well enough for both of us."

"I've never been this far away from home, Daddy."

"But I have."

"I don't know how we'll get there."

"But I do, and I'm the one taking you there."

After a while Lauren ran out of questions, but she still did not feel very secure about where we were going. The massive bridge over the Chesapeake Bay particularly frightened her as we approached it. Lauren had never before seen anything so large, and she was not convinced it was a good idea for us to cross it. Before she could begin questioning me again, I looked over at her and assured her, "Lauren, I didn't ask you to figure out how to cross the bridge, and I didn't ask you to go alone. I asked you to go with me, and you said you wanted to. I will take you where you need to be."

"Good night, Daddy."

"Good night, Lauren. I'll let you know when we get there."

Chapter Four

The Gift

What child does not enjoy receiving gifts from his or her father? When the relationship is healthy and strong, a gift from the father—even a small gift—is merely a visible extension of the love that is already resident. A father does not give gifts so he can be loved, but rather because love is already the core foundation of the bond between himself and his child.

A father who lives in a love relationship with his children gives according to both the need and the desire of his children. Jesus acknowledged as much in Matthew 7:9-11:

> Or what man is there among you, when his son shall ask for a loaf, will give him a stone? Or if he shall ask for a fish, he will not give him a snake, will he? If you then, being evil, know how to give good gifts to your children, how much more shall your Father who is in heaven give what is good to those who ask Him!

A gift is special when it originates from a love relationship with the father. It is special simply because the father knows.

As seen in the previous statements from Jesus, the mindset of a loving father giving good gifts is not foreign to one's Heavenly Father. In fact, God is vastly superior to even the best earthly fathers because of His divine nature and the total absence of evil from Him. As evident throughout the totality of Scripture, God is by nature the God who gives. While the New Testament contains other words for giving, one particular word utilizes the same Greek word for "grace" and describes the type of giving often associated with God. The word *charidzomai* means "to give graciously" or "to bestow

51

on one a favor or kindness." Scripture uses this word for the promises graciously given to Abraham (Gal. 3:18), of Jesus giving sight to many who were blind (Luke 7:21), as well as in graciously forgiving those who could in no way repay their debts (Luke 7:42).

The word *charidzomai* also repeatedly occurs concerning vital elements of salvation graciously given by God. Perhaps no better verse demonstrates this than Romans 8:32: "He who did not spare His own Son, but delivered Him up for us all, how will He not also with Him freely give [*charidzomai*] us all things?" Paul also employed it in describing how God gives believers His Holy Spirit so "we might know the things freely given [*charidzomai*] to us by God" (1 Cor. 2:12). Even spiritual gifts, so sought after and valued by so many, are, by definition, "grace gifts" (Rom. 12:6; 1 Cor. 12:9), being derived from the same root word *charidzomai*.

Scripture records another gift graciously given by God, but it is a gift no one requests. No one becomes envious when God bestows it on others, and no one anxiously awaits its arrival. Paul wrote to the Philippians of such a gift in one of the most intriguing statements in all Scripture: "For to you it has been granted/given [*charidzomai*] for Christ's sake, not only to believe in Him, but also to suffer for His sake" (Phil. 1:29). Paul utilized the same word for God giving suffering as he did for God giving His own Son to die (Rom. 8:32), as well as for the blessings associated with the Holy Spirit (1 Cor. 2:12). We gladly receive and welcome the first two given by God. On the other hand, not only do we not ask, we do not want "to be graciously given" suffering by God. Some "gift." When God gives us suffering, we would gladly return it and exchange it for something we really want, if we could ever get the heavenly store to open.

We have a difficult time harmonizing our theology with a verse that indicates God graciously gives suffering. It does not sound like Him, and it does not sound like us. If we were to visit friends in the hospital in intense suffering and inform them their suffering was a gracious gift from God, we would border on barbaric cruelty. Yet Paul writes this regarding the Philippians' suffering. It is not an apology because, after all, who apologizes for a gift? Paul by no means makes light of the Philippians' suffering, but neither does he pander to them. He does not issue forth, "Oh, you poor thing!" spoken by a sympathetic but bewildered bystander, someone whom we often search for when we suffer. We gladly receive such acknowledgment of our suffering and retire to lick our own wounds, thankful at least someone recognizes, cares, and understands—and by default we imply God does none of these.

Part of the reason we do not view suffering as originating from God is, from our earthly perspective, we do not associate it with good; we associate suffering with evil. We would hardly put suffering in the same category with other gifts we receive from God, such as freedom from the penalty of our sin or the refreshing elements of the fruit of the Spirit. Could we compare suffering with the gift of our admission into heaven? However, an even more foundational reason for our confusion is we view suffering as something Jesus did for us, and since He said, "It is finished!" we assume all suffering related to being God's child is finished as well. All that remains for us to do is to march joyfully and triumphantly throughout our life toward heaven, deeming ourselves removed and immune from the depths of suffering that afflict so many others throughout the world. After all, we have Jesus. However, when we meet with suffering—often intense suffering—our knees wobble and our hearts melt within us. We know God could intervene in our crisis, as He repeatedly has intervened before, but when He does not, we wonder what we have done to offend Him. If our suffering intensifies and becomes prolonged, as it often does, we wonder if God even knows how much we are suffering, and finally, we wonder if He even cares.

Still, Paul described suffering for Christ's sake in terms of God having granted or given a gift to the Philippians. We should note the suffering Paul spoke of applies only to Christians. Others throughout the world suffer every day, some more extremely than we ever will experience. Theirs may be a suffering that leads one to salvation, or sadly, it may not. Suffering is hard enough without having any eternal consequence derived from it. What Paul writes about is suffering as a Christian, indeed, even suffering specifically because you are a Christian. An aspect of such suffering may be persecution, but it is not at all limited to this realm. In other words, suffering of this nature would not come upon you unless you were already in a love relationship with the Heavenly Father. It cannot lead you to God because you are already united with Him in Christ. It is not something you could even bring about by your own volition because, after all, if you initiated it or took it upon yourself, it would no longer be a gift. Since Paul presented the suffering of the Philippians as a gracious gift from God, and since most of us consider such suffering as anything but a gift, it must come down to a matter of definition and perspective—as do most good things from God.

<hr>

As before, with any area of Scripture, it is our responsibility to drop down into the world of the original participants and "see with their eyes and hear with their ears." Then we examine the truths established and consider how they relate to us. Let's begin with the Apostle Paul.

Few people know suffering to the degree Paul did. At his conversion the ascended Jesus described Paul as "a chosen instrument of Mine, to bear My name before the Gentiles and kings and the sons of Israel; for I will show him how much he must suffer for My name's sake" (Acts 9:15-16). Of course, Jesus always knows of what He speaks. Long before Paul completed his ministry he described some of the particulars of his sufferings in his second epistle to the Corinthians. Many Corinthian believers there had succumbed to the heretical teaching of false apostles. Paul—who founded the church and then undertook manual labor at Corinth to pay his own expense, taking nothing from the Corinthians for his ministry among them—was forced by the Corinthians to defend his own motives, integrity, and qualifications for his self-sacrificing ministry among them. The Corinthians should have been ashamed of themselves, but those who are spiritually arrogant and mere babes in the faith rarely, if ever, are. Without going into specifics, Paul described some of the events that accompanied his walk with the Lord. Again 2 Corinthians 11:23-27 gives a broad account of Paul's suffering:

> Are they [the false apostles] servants of Christ? (I speak as if insane), I more so; in far more labors, in far more imprisonments, beaten times without number, often in danger of death. Five times I received from the Jews thirty-nine lashes. Three times I was beaten with rods, once I was stoned, three times I was shipwrecked, a night and a day I have spent in the deep. I have been on frequent journeys, in danger from robbers, dangers from my countrymen, dangers from the Gentiles, dangers in the city, dangers in the wilderness, dangers on the sea, dangers among false brethren; I have been in labor and hardship, through many sleepless nights, in hunger and thirst, often without food, in cold and exposure.

Notice Paul did not have much company during many of these events, as seen with the use of "I" instead of "we." Loneliness no doubt made his suffering more intense. So much for the "Prosperity Gospel" that teaches God wants you wealthy, healthy, and happy, and if these characteristics are not yours, it is your own fault because you lack the necessary faith. Actually, exactly the opposite is true. It takes exceedingly more faith to endure such hostilities for the sake of Christ and to continue walking with the Lord. It would be interesting to see how many of those who hold this teaching would still be with Paul—let alone with God—after they endured merely one of the hardships Paul suffered.

So when Paul writes to the Philippians of suffering, and presents their suffering as being given by God, he speaks of firsthand experience, and as very few Christians throughout the centuries could speak. In fact, Paul could write "it has been given to you not only to believe but also to suffer" only after he himself had repeatedly experienced the same hardships and witnessed its beneficial results in his own life. Paul became a visible demonstration of how God used suffering for the Philippians' invisible faith. He could properly recognize the source and reason for the suffering of the Philippians and encourage them accordingly. This may partly explain why God often gives suffering to those He loves. Those who suffer under the Lord's design do so not only for what it does for them, but also as a means of God's grace extended to others. Paul had previously explained to the Corinthians, "Blessed be the God and Father of our Lord Jesus Christ, the Father of mercies and God of all comfort; who comforts us in all our affliction so that we may be able to comfort those who are in any affliction with the comfort with which we ourselves are comforted by God" (2 Cor. 1:3-4). Paul elsewhere wrote that believers are created in Christ Jesus for good works (Eph. 2:10). Part of the good works may be God's use of suffering in our own life, coupled with the lessons learned from them, to encourage and strengthen other believers who are just stepping into the arena of suffering, much the same way Paul did for the Philippians.

Acts 16 reveals the founding of the church at Philippi was due, in a large degree, to how Paul and Silas responded to their own suffering. After having been severely beaten for their Christian witness and then painfully having their feet locked in stocks in prison, they did something totally inconsistent with the world's value system: They sang songs of praise to God (Acts 16:25). I wonder what we would have sung in that prison.

I wonder if being there would elicit praise to God or grumblings because of our circumstances and our perceived abandonment by God. Acts 16:25 concludes by noting "and the prisoners were listening to them." Such songs of praise were incongruous with the surroundings and the events of the day. The response of Paul and Silas to suffering impressed the Philippian jailer and others to such a degree they sought after such a magnificent God who wondrously had control over earthly events and people—and the church at Philippi was born. This leads to a second revelatory beam of light from the Lord: When one endures suffering for the sake of Christ, and even demonstrates joy in the midst of suffering, the world takes notice. They may not fully understand it, or even appreciate it, but they most assuredly will notice. Joyful endurance speaks more loudly for the reality of a loving and powerful God than do rallies, buildings, programs, polish and pizzazz. The problem is it is often so rarely found today.

Some may think God uses suffering only in the lives of spiritual super-stars such as the Apostle Paul. However, suffering is in no way limited only to "full-time Christian workers" or for those in church leadership positions. God readily gives this gift to any of His children, the degree being determined as the Father in His unfathomable wisdom sees fit. This becomes evident when one considers the churches of Macedonia. In writing to the Corinthians—who were experts in Christian receiving—Paul used the Macedonian churches as examples of Christian giving. The churches of Macedonia were extremely good churches by biblical standards. They consisted of the Thessalonians "who received the word in much tribulation, with the joy of the Holy Spirit" (1 Thess. 1:6), and the Bereans, who "were more noble-minded than [the unbelievers] in Thessalonica, for they received the word with great eagerness, examining the Scriptures daily, to see whether these things were so" (Acts 17:11). The Macedonian churches also included the church at Philippi. However, these churches consisted of more than doctrinal studies and withstanding persecution. The effects of Christ in their lives showed up repeatedly, especially in their sacrificial giving. Paul wrote of them "that in a great ordeal of affliction their abundance of joy and their deep poverty overflowed in the wealth of their liberality, begging us with much entreaty for the favor of participation in the support of the saints" (2 Cor. 8:2-4). Who would not like to be a member of such a church where God's grace so freely flowed?

We must look not so much at what the Macedonian churches gave, but rather at what they had, or even more to the point, what they did not have. For one thing, the believers at Macedonia "were in a great deal of affliction," which is another way of saying they themselves were suffering. Instead of murmuring and complaining, they repeatedly sought opportunity to give to others and bring glory to God. Macedonia had formerly been a rather wealthy area with many gold and silver mines. However, at this time in history the Roman Empire had confiscated the mines. Poverty became extensive in the area. Paul's terminology describes just how poor these believers were. He writes of "their deep poverty." The word "deep" is the Greek word *bathos*, where we get our word "bath." It originally meant "down to the depth," or in modern terminology, "rock bottom." The poverty of the Macedonian churches was such that it could not get any lower than it already was. In fact, the word "poverty" [*ptocheia*] depicts abject poverty in which one has virtually nothing and is in imminent danger of real starvation. In 2 Corinthians 8:9 Paul twice used this word in reference to the totality of Jesus' giving of Himself: "that though He was rich, yet for your sake He became poor [*ptocheia*], that you through His poverty [*ptocheia*] might become rich." These faithful believers did not know where they were going to get the money for their daily sustenance, even for their own families. However, these churches were full of people corresponding to the widow who gave her last two cents to the Lord—and corresponding to the Lord Jesus Christ Himself. (Do you still want to be a member there?) The Macedonian believers did not revel in their misery, and they did not repeatedly question God with the never-ending "why?" regarding their own problems. Not only did they give, but also they continued giving and gave joyfully. They repeatedly entreated Paul so they could give to others they deemed more in need than they considered themselves, and they gave above and beyond themselves. No doubt heaven took notice.

The world, though, probably would not notice the Macedonian churches, especially many of today's Christian world. Because of the depth of their poverty, the Macedonian churches would not be of much value in attaining the bottom-line amount of money "needed" for Christian causes and organizations. If you needed $1,000, the Macedonians collectively might have been able to scrape together $10. The Philippians would not be solicited with request letters from Christian ministries. What they gave would hardly cover the cost of postage. The Macedonian church members would not be considered for board member vacancies in Christian institutions because they obviously knew little regarding how the world worked, although their understanding of how God worked was quite deep and growing. They had nothing to offer and everything to offer—it all depends on your values and perspective.

The Philippian church would most likely not attract many modern day Christian church-hunters either. It would hardly be recognized amid the clutter of many churches today, simply because they did not have enough money to buy any clutter. One who visited them may have surmised, "They have nothing to offer me. They simply do not meet my needs. They're nice people, but their facilities are lacking. They don't even have a gymnasium to entertain my children. Obviously, God does not want me to be a part of such a small group. Besides, their limited size clearly shows their lack of vision for ministry and their lack of commitment to God. If they had more of these qualities, maybe God would bless them more." And no doubt heaven once more takes notice.

So when Paul wrote to the Philippians he did not write to them concerning stress, Christian finances, how to find fulfillment in life, fun activities for the youth, or "how to write your own ticket with God"—the title of a chapter in a book I saw at a Christian bookstore. He did not send a Christian calendar or a Pauline pinup. He did not distribute an advertising circular detailing his own itinerary, including the necessary financial information required for him to make a personal appearance. Even beyond all these, Paul never appealed to the Philippians for help with his own dire circumstances, which were often equally or even more dismal than those of the Philippians, especially since he himself was in prison when he wrote to them. He wrote simply as one sojourner in suffering to a fellowship of sojourning sufferers, and together they embraced a deeper bond than most believers will ever experience on earth.

You can gauge your own spiritual depth by seeing whether any of the following questions reside in your own heart. Would you want to be a member of the Macedonian churches? Would you be able to give to others under such circumstances, or would you see that as an infringement on what you view as yours? If God caused the same circumstances in your life—or worse—would you consider yourself blessed of God or abandoned by Him? Could you continue walking with Jesus in the depth of isolated darkness, or is your walk merely reserved for brightly lit days overflowing with the blessings of God? Perhaps the most penetrating questions are often those which we would never audibly voice, especially in the presence of other believers: "But if these churches gave themselves so completely to the Lord, then why would God not bless them in return? They gave to God, so isn't God obligated to give back to them in return? It seems as though God delights in taking what little they had, and He gave them little, if anything, in return. Instead of getting easier, their lives became harder the deeper the Macedonian Christians walked with the Lord. Maybe it would be better for me not to be so radical in my relationship with God. After all, if He is going to take everything, I'm not sure I'm ready to follow. I'm not sure I can handle this 'gift' from God." As before, it all depends on your definition of blessing, and it all depends on your perspective.

The Macedonian churches had already formulated their viewpoint on giving to and receiving from God, which is why they gave so freely, even in the midst of intense suffering. Paul disclosed the secret of such a mindset in 2 Corinthians 8:5: "but they first gave themselves to the Lord." Again, the irony of true Christian giving shows itself. God does not want or need our money; He wants us. If He has us—our hearts, our passion, our drive—then money is no problem. Neither is time or commitment or sacrifice or inconvenience or suffering or walking by faith contrary to the world's methodology. When one first gives oneself to the Lord, the allurements of the world become less and less attractive and increasingly shallower. Not only this, but when an individual or a church gives themselves to the Lord, it is not so much characterized by ethereal sighings before God, but rather it becomes evident in their relationship with others around them. Sacrificial giving to others becomes as natural a correspondence as exhaling is to inhaling. In its simplest terms, when the Macedonia churches "first gave themselves to the Lord," it meant all which the world—even those in the Christian world—values and lecherously clings to was replaced by an all-encompassing desire to know Christ in a deeper and ever-increasing fashion. God blessed and honored such a desire to know Him on a level oblivious to most believers, and the results continue throughout eternity.

Paul understood this mindset and later used it in his appeal to the Philippians in other areas of their Christian walk. While he wrote of the Macedonians giving themselves to the Lord, it was equally or even abundantly true of him. He demonstrated this by the consistency of his walk with Jesus. He also opened his heart to the Philippians and allowed them—and us—a peek inside at the sweetness of the fellowship he knew with Jesus—and how we can share in that same fellowship too.

Chapter Five

The Fellowship

About six weeks after our twins died, I received a call asking me to perform a funeral. Although I had been in the ministry for years, I never grew accustomed to funerals. I often thought how ironic it was I had only attended four funerals my entire life before I officiated at my first one. I went through a period of almost ten years when no family members or friends died. I would have attended my grandfather's funeral, but my appendix ruptured the day he died. I thought I had more than made up for lost time in that I did nearly thirty funerals in a three-year period.

But this funeral was different. For one thing, I was in the midst of my own grief. Often, as a pastor you must "wear" the grief of others. I did not know whether I was ready to step into someone else's grief while bringing my own heartache to the family. Another difference was that this funeral was for a man in his early thirties who had died from a brain tumor. He was the youngest child in the family, and that made it extremely difficult to agree to do the funeral. You expect in the normal flow of life that your parents will die before you. When your children die ahead of you, it seems to be an unnatural act against God's standard order, and there is no good comparison to make to it. Having one's child die is not similar to friends dying or even a brother and sister dying. While each of these stab with their own deep wells of loss, the death of your child stands alone.

So I did not know what to do when the family, whom I never met before, asked me to do their son's funeral. My initial reaction was to run away as fast and far as I could. I had two compelling fears. First, grieving is a process, and mine was nowhere near complete. I dreaded the thought of re-opening my own wounds as I encountered the sorrow of the family members, particularly the parents. As mentioned, my appendix ruptured the day my grandfather died. After this occurred there was a fifty-fifty chance the surgeon would have to perform a second operation in a day or two to remove damaged tissue. Second operations are usually much harder to bear because you are already depleted physically. The mental dread of it also wears you down. This is precisely how I felt about overseeing this funeral. I dreaded it worse than I did a second operation. My wound of grief was far too fresh, the cut too deep not to bleed freely again at even the slightest provocation.

My second major concern was I did not know whether I had the composure to officiate at the funeral, let alone meet the family at the funeral home. When you begin the grieving process, different items spark deep weeping. I likened grief to a poison being removed from my body with tears being the channel of exit. Especially at the early stages of grief, I never knew what would set it off: a song, a hug, a memory, a smell, the sadness on someone's face—anything. I felt that I would be microscopically exposed to the hundreds who would attend, and I did not want to break down during the funeral. It was not so much the embarrassment of crying in public I feared, but rather not knowing whether I could make it through the funeral that gave me pause.

Although I do not know exactly why, I agreed to do the funeral. Parts of the endeavor were just as I expected; others were not. As I drove to the funeral home, the freshness of the twins' death overcame me as I wept the entire way. Strangely though, I never cried at the funeral home. I got out of the car to meet the family for the first time, thinking that it must be a similar feeling as one walking to his own execution. Rubber legs with anchor shoes somehow transported me there. The funeral director escorted me to where the family sat, and when I saw them, I understood why I had agreed to do the funeral: I *had* to do it. While I knew of friends throughout the world who could address the need and minister greatly, I knew of nobody else in the immediate area who could minister from an experiential standpoint. This poor lady had lost her baby boy; her husband, his youngest son; and Betsy and I, the twins. It does not matter if your baby is thirty years old or one day old, losing a child goes beyond description. You have to "be there" to understand it fully—and the family and I were.

Since I had only attended four funerals my entire life, I often felt like an intruder even when I received requests to officiate. I was in my mid-thirties at the time, and I did not take lightly the fact that I did funerals for people who lost their lifetime mates, some married for twenty years longer than I had been alive. What does a young preacher have to say to someone in a realm of grief of which he has no experiential understanding? At times, it seemed almost farcical. I simply felt as though I did not belong there; I felt I invaded others' private world of grief. The death of the twins changed that. Not that I was the greatest griever ever, but I did understand grief so much better than before. I have never felt out of place since then, and it began with meeting the family of the young man who died. While I could not explain why or anything else about the death of their son, I could look them in the eye and tell them God loves them. I could speak from the heart of Christ's great love and concern for them, and that He was the only source of comfort during so great a loss. I did tell them, as the fraternity of sufferers gained a few more members that day.

I left the funeral home picking up my rubber legs and anchor shoes as I laboriously made my way back to the car and the grief that awaited me. I had not cried when I visited the family. It was as though God allowed me a temporary haven as I dealt with the family, only to be engulfed again in the cloak of sorrow as I drove home. While I made it through the initial encounter with the family, I still was not sure I could do the funeral.

Then it hit me—I had to do the funeral. I had focused so much on the initial meeting with the family I had forgotten that I was to address a few hundred people who would be attending in two days. What do you say to the family and others present? How do you show God's love and grace after their son died? How do you as "God's representative" represent God accurately in a situation that causes many to question the existence of God, and even more so His love?

A few weeks before the twins died I had attended a funeral for the sister of a friend of mine. A secular psychiatrist was the main speaker. He told how the one dead was not really dead but lived on in immortality through the memories of those who knew her. No comfort accompanies this, even if it were true, I thought to myself. In a relatively brief time those who remember her will likewise die. If immortality only consists of "living on in our thoughts and heart," her immortality will fade as one by one those who remember her die, until ultimately no one living will remember her. Not exactly a biblical concept of immortality; not exactly a scenario of hope. The speaker went on to inform the gatherers how the deceased lived on in spirit. "Whenever you see a child's smiling face," he said, "she is present. She is there with the golden sunset. Her spirit will surround you when you smell the garden flowers after a spring rain," and on it went. Of course, this was merely one man's futile attempt to salvage some good out of death's cold reality. What he did in a sense was deny the reality and finality of death, attempting to disguise it by incorporating death into the pleasant scenarios of life. He stated no truth in what he said and also in what he did not say. While there are moments when children smile, sunsets are viewed, and fresh smells please the senses, life also contains other events not so lovely: the diagnosis of a lifelong disease, being informed that the tumor is malignant, receiving the news of the car wreck that killed a family of five. If this lady were present at the good things of life, I thought, I wonder what prevented her from accompanying the bad ones. I think the grievers left the funeral even more burdened than when they arrived. The psychiatrist offered no hope, nor did he address the deep grief of the heart. I came away saddened no one presented God and His Word. I knew of no other solace to offer.

Now it was my turn to conduct another funeral. It was the first one I did since I attended the secular funeral a few months earlier. I was not sure exactly how to approach the message. Knowing what not to say, such as the ethereal-based sentiments of a secular psychiatrist, is not the same as knowing what to say, especially with the death of a young man. I never referred to funeral manuals with the other funerals I did, believing God used His own Word to comfort as no other source does. This funeral could be no different, but then again, what do you say? I wrestled over this all day and night, simultaneously struggling with my own grief in the midst of the preparations. It was a strange mixture of preparing to minister in the name of the Lord while at the same time receiving grace and comfort from God and His Word. The night before the funeral I knew what I was to say. I still did not know whether I could say it without weeping.

The black cloud of grief accompanied me as I drove to the funeral, and then again, no doubt by God's grace, it lifted as I arrived at the funeral home. While the funeral was by no means easy, and not once did I feel at ease during it, I did sense God's power as I stood up to speak. I limited my remarks to three items. I agreed with the wordless sentiments of those present—how difficult it was to see God's hand and love in the death of a young man. However, such heart-rending perplexity was nothing new.

Wanting to know why such tragedies occur has been an ongoing ache of mankind from earliest history. Often we who remain reason we somehow must be the ones ultimately responsible for such a humanly unexplainable tragedy. Jesus knows this. When Jesus and the disciples encountered a man born blind, the disciples had a logical question: Who sinned, the man or the man's parents? They assumed such misery must be directly related to the sins of someone, and they wanted to know who was to blame. The answer Jesus gave is at once both startling and comforting. In John 9:3 Jesus answered, "It was neither that this man sinned, nor his parents; but it was in order that the works of God might be displayed in him." We, too, must trust that answer. When someone dear to us dies—especially a child—we can scan the long list of sins and shortcomings we have committed and conclude it must be God's hand of retribution against one of our more heinous acts. What grace God gives as He calls us to look to Him instead of the unfathomable mysteries of sorrow and grief. What comfort in knowing we are not the cause of the death. God knows our beginning and our end from before the foundation of the world. He numbers our days by His sovereign counsel. While we should never take sin lightly or assume consequences do not follow our actions, we must look to a greater hope. Our focus should be on the promise of God that "neither this man sinned, nor his parents"—and look instead for God to display His works.

That biblical truth led to the second point. I told those present that God knows firsthand what it is like to watch His own child die—and, even more amazing—He possessed the power to prevent His child's death at any time. We who watch our children die and cannot intervene have it much easier. What an incomparable demonstration of God's love to restrain Himself from intervention as His Son, Jesus Christ, hung dying for the sins of the world. God's lack of intervention opened the way so we could have access and fellowship with Him—but it cost God dearly. Parents naturally value their children above all else; we simply mimic this from observing God's love of Jesus. I would gather from Jesus' death that God must have a special grace and sympathy for parents who experience the same loss. I also gave a brief Gospel presentation. It was vital those at the funeral understand the eternal difference between hearing the Gospel of God's love versus actually praying to receive Jesus.

Finally, I read the letter I had written about the twins, found in the opening chapter of this book. Most people attending the funeral did not know of my situation until then. I told them I came there that day as a pilgrim and sojourner in grief, a beggar in need of God's grace. As Peter said to the lame man, "Silver and gold have I none, but such as I have, I give unto you." The "such as I have" was God's mercy, grace, and peace, not from earthly sources, but originating from the divine Trinity. It was the loving truth that the dead son did not live on in the smell of a flower, but lived in the love and care provided by His loving heavenly Father. (The one who died was a Christian, being saved a few years before his death. His testimony in enduring cancer tremendously affected many.) I told those present the stark truth that the resulting sorrow is too much to endure alone. God wants to be a part of their grieving as well. He wants to be the source of comfort and hope to all who ask Him. They knew I hurt with them, and I believe they understood God hurt with them too. I made it through the funeral, burial, and the dozens of people I spoke with after the service. I returned to my car—and to my shroud of grief—and wept all the way home. I collapsed in bed and slept the deep sleep of the exhausted.

In a sense, we entered a fellowship that day. An aspect of the fellowship was the grieving family and myself. In a unique way, a fellowship between God and others also began, at least in its rudimentary stage. I do not know how many, if any, received Christ that day, but I do know they understood God's love better. If nothing else, I think God planted the seeds for deeper and fuller fellowship with Him. Many who attended perceived God's sorrow instead of assuming His cold absence. I will find out the rest when I get to heaven. I know they viewed God as present and active—as He truly is—and I know they heard God desired fellowship with them.

"God desired fellowship with them"—and with us—what an awe-inspiring concept. For those who already know the Lord, the word "fellowship" usually conjures warm sentiment. Lack of fellowship with God is a mysterious ache for those who do not commune with Him. Many know their lives lack something, and that something is the presence of a personal relationship with God. Fellowship with Him is a fundamental need of the human condition; God created us so.

The Greek word *koinonia*, generally translated "fellowship," also means "participation, association, communion, sharers in." The word did not originate in the Christian world. Secular writings of the day used *koinonia* with roughly the same definition. However, with the birth of the Church, and primarily through the Holy Spirit, the word portrayed a unique and warm fellowship, a fellowship of unity in Christ. Strangely enough *koinonia* is completely absent from the Gospel accounts. Perhaps this is so the focus can be properly on the unique person and work of Jesus. John 1:14 records, "and the word became flesh and dwelt [or "tabernacled"] among us." God incarnate in the flesh living among His creation was magnificent in itself, but still a void existed until Jesus completed our redemption. Full fellowship with God was only in the process of being opened when Jesus lived on the earth. However, a vital change in relation transpired after the resurrection. Later in John 20:17 the risen Jesus told Mary Magdalene, "Go to My brethren, and say to them, 'I ascend to My Father and your Father, and My God and your God.'" This is the first instance in Scripture where Jesus ever referred to the disciples as his "brethren." Before He had only tabernacled in their midst, now they were sharers in Him, participants with Him—His brethren. In other words, Jesus established fellowship that day, and an eternal fellowship at that.

However, Christ did not restrict this new fellowship only to the original disciples, nor only in their relationship to God. Jesus expanded fellowship to include anyone from this point onward whom He would save and who would become part of His church. The Body of Christ was and is living. His church is not an organization but instead a living entity. Fellowship would, of course, be with God, but also be with true believers everywhere. Not only would fellowship be available, it should be operative if the church and her members are to have a spiritually healthy relationship. Acts 2:42, the first instance of *koinonia* recorded in Scripture, demonstrates the necessity of such communion: "And they [the believers in the early church] were continually devoting themselves to the apostles' teaching and to fellowship (*koinonia*), to the breaking of bread and to prayer." This passage contains four vital components of the early church, and *koinonia* fellowship is among them. Fellowship was not only what they possessed, but to what they continually devoted themselves; they nurtured it.

The Apostle Paul frequently used *koinonia*, but always in the new Christian sense, never its secular use. Paul knew Christ was the basis for fellowship, and His fellowship showed up in diverse areas. Paul wrote of Godward aspects in "the fellowship with His Son" (1 Cor. 1:9), "the fellowship of the Holy Spirit" (2 Cor. 13:14), and "the fellowship [participation] of the Gospel" (Phil. 1:5). Fellowship could also signify full acceptance of another. That Peter, James, and John extended "the right hand of fellowship" to Paul greatly encouraged him as these three key figures openly recognized the apostolic ministry given to him (Gal. 2:9). They would never hastily approve anyone for something as strategic as an apostle's ministry, especially Paul, since he once persecuted the Body of Christ. Even in addressing the fellowship of a dear friend, Paul still realized the basis went vastly beyond earthly association. He wrote in Philemon 6, "I pray that the fellowship of your faith may become effective through the knowledge of every good thing which is in you for Christ's sake." In Paul's estimation, fellowship began with God but carried over to personal relations within the Church. The same holds true today. Fellowship begins with God—not with others. Those who skip over the Cornerstone to enjoy "religious fellowship" with each other based on their own merits simply have a form of godliness, but they deny the power therein.

One verse yet remains where Paul wrote of fellowship, but its use we do not expect. Paul wrote of Jesus in Philippians 3:10, "That I may know Him, and the power of His resurrection and the fellowship of His sufferings, being conformed to His death." Paul's use of *koinonia* for sharing in the sufferings of Christ is as surprising as "God's gift of suffering" earlier in Philippians 1:29. Not only did Paul know such sufferings existed, he actively sought fellowship with Jesus in the midst of them. Most of us do not respond that way. Maybe we should explore why Paul would write such a statement and see whether it helps us in our understanding of suffering.

Paul wrote to the Philippians while living under house arrest in Rome. While that may not sound as bad as the restraints of a dark dungeon, being in house prison under Roman guard for two years must have been extremely burdensome for one who had stayed on the move as much as Paul did. Paul spread the Gospel over much of Asia and Europe, establishing numerous churches and patiently building up the believers in the faith. At this juncture, however, God removed him from his previous decades of work. For a while Paul would no longer be the traveling missionary. Instead, God set Paul aside for an important function. In addition to Paul speaking with several who visited him at his Roman dwelling, God strategically used this time to bring about the writings of Ephesians, Colossians, Philemon, and Philippians. The Church continues to benefit from the fruit of Paul's two-year Roman imprisonment.

Paul had approximately two years or less to live when he wrote Philippians—and what a life it had been! From his early days of Jewish prosperity Paul abandoned all to follow the Lord Jesus Christ wherever He led. But had it been worth it? Was Paul's life a grand success or blatant failure? Would one argue success for a prisoner with only a few months left to live? Would you apply the same standard of evaluation to your own life and be pleased? It all depends on one's criteria.

From casual observation by the world's standards, Paul's life was anything but a grand success. Associates who knew Paul from his days as a Pharisee would only refer to him after a disdainful huff. "Paul—or better Saul, as I knew him; I will not subscribe the fictitious new name he now employs—had everything and more than six lifetimes could hope for. Although I never cared for him personally and would not consider him my friend, I cannot deny the God of Heaven gave him a sound mind. So what did he do with it? What good or service did he perform for our God or our people? I will tell you what he did: The brilliant young rabbi renounced his status, family, heritage, and yes, even his God—and for what? To align himself with a convicted and executed felon whom he somehow perceives to be the Christ. The Son of God crucified? Our Messiah? It is a wonder Heaven itself does not consume him at once for his blasphemy. Even more amusing, if it were not so pathetic, is that Saul himself used to arrest entire families who held to the same myth. His actions led to their imprisonment, torture, or execution—and now he has become one of them. Even worse, Saul has for most intents and purposes become a Gentile, those cursed dogs who defy God above and defile our people. May God Almighty destroy them all, including their little puppet 'Paul.'"

"So what has been the outcome of this mystical chase of Saul's Messiah? Does Saul sit in the Sanhedrin? Is he a teacher at an established school? Do his countrymen revere him? No, he traverses all Asia and Europe, only repeatedly to be abused, mocked, beaten, and imprisoned in the various cities he enters, often even by his own countrymen. Scarcely any part of his body has escaped the whips and rods inflicted on him by those he deemed needed enlightening. He has no home and no family, and in reality, no country. His last visit here in Jerusalem led to such a riot, I doubt Saul will be permitted to return by either Jews or Romans. Even now I hear he is imprisoned in Rome waiting to speak before Caesar, of all people. Does Saul think he, in chain and common thread, will impress the leader of what the Gentiles call the glory of Rome? I would laugh in his face. I will tell you this: If Saul does not desist from his inane and controversial diatribe, the authorities will most assuredly rid themselves of this diminutive pest. What a waste. What a profane waste of one's life and capabilities. Some Christ you follow, 'Paul.' Some Son of God. Saul has lost everything. He has nothing."

The externals of the previous scenario were true: Paul had suffered great loss. But what did his heart contain? Any regrets, Paul? Would you do it over the same way if you could? When you are by yourself at night, do your thoughts linger over what might have been if you had remained a Pharisee? Did you ever wish for a son? Do you miss the loving embrace of a wife? Satan may have whispered, "You know, Paul, you had everything before. Look at what all the others have, including so-called followers of Jesus! *You have nothing!*" If such thoughts ever traversed his mind, they would find no home there. Paul did not view himself as a loser but a gainer. In Philippians 3 he acknowledged his prestigious background no longer existed. Yet, he concluded in 3:7-8,

> But whatever things were gain to me, those things I have counted as a loss for the sake of Christ. More than that I count all things to be loss in view of the surpassing value of knowing Christ Jesus my Lord, for whom I have suffered the loss of all things, and count them but rubbish in order that I may gain Christ.

He had lost everything—but he had gained Life. By Paul's calculation, he was more than content with the transaction.

Paul wrote more. Even though he had relatively little time left to live, he did not consider his work finished. What is more important, Paul did not view himself as having arrived spiritually. Always striving ahead, always learning, always relentlessly pursuing—Him. While Paul was a scholastic genius, his relationship with Jesus never consisted of information or mere academic accumulation. The doctrinal truths were essential, but they emerged from a living Person, and Paul kept Him at the forefront of his life and pursuits. Although he had walked with the Lord for decades and probably knew Him better than anyone alive, Paul wanted more. The drive of his life was to know Jesus in an ever-increasing way, in an ever-deepening fellowship.

If you asked most Christians today what it would take for them to know Jesus better, the answers most likely would range from Bible study, time alone with God, prayer, a good church, good fellowship, seminars, or Christian magazines. Most of these have varying validity, but in Paul's estimation, they lacked a key component. In Philippians 3:10 Paul wrote that I may "know Him." He used the Greek word that generally means, "to know by experience," rather than "to know intellectually." Herein is a foundational difference between Paul and many others. Some limit their knowledge of Jesus only to information. Scribble it in a notebook, take good notes, treat the Bible as an academic textbook—walk away and leave it when you want. For Paul, the Person of Jesus stayed in the forefront. He never denied the need for deep study—he enjoyed it—but he never divorced doctrine from the Author. Living words from the living God nourished Paul throughout his Christian walk.

Paul added two aspects of what knowing Jesus entailed: the power of His resurrection and the fellowship of His sufferings. Most of us delight in seeing "the power of His resurrection" in our lives. It is thrilling beyond words to see the mighty hand of God in action working powerfully and precisely as He delivers us from many perils and predicaments, or brings victory against all odds. But Paul did not stop there—nor should we. He connected "the power of His resurrection" and "the fellowship of His sufferings" with the word "and." You cannot divide and separate them, each component being similar to two sides of one coin; you don't have one face without the other. Paul did not merely want to know the power—power can be impersonal, as can knowledge. He wanted to know the fellowship of the sufferings. This last phrase is important. Paul was not a masochist who desired to know suffering for suffering's sake. He needed no additional suffering to impress others or show off his commitment to Jesus above all others. Nowhere in Scripture did Paul ask or seek to suffer, nor should we.

Most of us do not count the same way as Paul did either. Paul counted all things as a loss for the sake of knowing Christ. Most of us limit our counting to one: We want to know the power of Christ's resurrection. The fellowship of His suffering does not interest us, and left to our own inclinations, we would avoid it at all costs. Not Paul. He did not want to see only the power of Jesus; he wanted to know Him—to know experientially, be a firsthand witness, not a reader of someone else's experience with Him. Paul desired the fellowship, not merely the display of power. The difference is similar to Moses' personal fellowship with God versus the Hebrew wanderers who witnessed God's glory from a distance. The glory of God is magnificent, and we should be glad when God grants us opportunity to see bits of it displayed, but it is incomplete. To know Him and the fellowship of His sufferings requires a stronger commitment, a deeper walk—but what riches await.

This is Paul's second reference to suffering in Philippians. Earlier in 1:29 Paul wrote, "For to you it has been granted [graciously given] for Christ's sake, not only to believe in Him, but also to suffer for His sake." Now he wrote of the fellowship of Christ's sufferings. If one has suffered greatly, these verses bring encouragement. If one never has, these verses make little sense. Most do not see suffering as a gift from God or as part of the process of a deeper Christian walk. Many of us are at the point where we want Jesus—and we want the things He gives. For most of us it remains a lifelong battle for balance, especially if family members look to you to provide. While worldly pursuits cannot keep us from Jesus if we are saved, they can and do keep us from knowing Him as deeply as He desires. We are as the two disciples on the road to Emmaus who beckon Jesus to come dine with us, even when it seems He would go farther. We—not He—put on the brakes, content with a surface knowledge of Him, satisfied with the perishable prizes we of the world only rent, but never truly possess. Suffering helps us in this regard because it forces (or even takes) things from us—often good things. If responded to properly (and that is not at all a given), suffering forces us to find comfort and mercy in present fellowship with Jesus, and look to Him for hope for the future. Suffering makes the world less a sphere where we feel at home, and heaven a much more definitive reality. However, if you are looking for your heaven on earth, you will be extremely disappointed with God. Suffering loosens our ties with the present world, and fertilizes our desire to be home with the Lord.

You can usually tell in commentaries when one writes about "the fellowship of His sufferings" from a purely intellectual versus experiential capacity. For one thing, usually the comments are brief. It is though it is best to move on to another subject, especially since Paul wrote suffering is a gift of God, and this gift may arrive at any unexpected moment. Some seem ill at ease with this passage, describing suffering in terms as foreign to them as we would describe walking on the moon. We may have an intellectual idea of what it would be like on the moon, but we do not sense the crunch of the ground beneath our feet, or how the change in gravity feels to our stomach. We may have a marginal understanding, but we do not know by experience. We have not been present there. Neither have many who comment on biblical verses about suffering. Many portray "the fellowship of His sufferings" as an automatic process, and seem to equate it with the daily hardships of life. Do not unbelievers also have daily hardships, suffering, sorrow, and financial pressures? Others write of this as "the suffering which all Christians must endure," or "tribulations common to every Christian," and equate these with a one-size-fits-all sweater to be worn. Those who write about suffering—but not out of suffering—usually refer to the fellowship of the sufferings of Christ in all-encompassing statement, supported by little if any corresponding example, and hurriedly move on to the next subject. It is not a comfortable place to park. Even more so, explaining suffering to others goes beyond intellectual explanation, and enduring suffering stretches both the intellect and especially one's faith.

Actually, not all Christians suffer to the same degree. Part of the reason is because of our choice not to know Him better. The pursuits and distractions of the world are ample hindrances themselves, let alone any attacks from Satan, that will cause us to give up on God and not walk in darkness. Another part is because of God's infinite and precise knowledge of us. Paul wrote that God would not allow us to be tempted beyond what we are able. God knows how much each one of us can take, and for some, especially those content on a surface knowledge of Him and those very much at home in the world, maybe the extent of their suffering is their car breaking down or a withered summer lawn. God still loves them, but He knows they could not endure. While I'm not totally sure about this, and I by no means say I speak for God, it still goes back to what Paul wrote to the Philippians, instructing them that suffering was a gift. The carnal-minded Corinthians "were not lacking in any [spiritual] gift" (1 Cor. 1:7). They had relatively little suffering, but they also possessed only a surface knowledge of Jesus. The Philippians, on the other hand, had little of God's external blessing. Instead, they received God's gift of suffering, and out of this harvested a deep walk and fellowship with their Savior. God knew who could endure what. Earthly assessment never equates with eternal design and consequences. This does not mean if one does not suffer they lack commitment to or depth of fellowship with Jesus. Rather it simply views suffering from a different vantage point, observing that suffering can be used of God for His purposes, especially to know Him in a manner we never knew existed.

But, exactly what does "the fellowship of His sufferings" mean? We know it cannot refer to Christ's sacrificial death. Jesus alone atoned for sin; He alone became our High Priest. Simply put, knowing the fellowship of His sufferings means you know Him better—not know about Him better. It is similar to understanding your parents better after you have children. You have an experiential base—and often vastly more appreciation—because you realize the sacrificial labor of love involved in raising children. Often, we in our suffering question whether God knows or cares. We want others to know what it is like for us. The fellowship of His suffering is just the opposite: We learn what it was like for Him. We understand Him more and walk away with a clearer definition and greater appreciation of His love. While no doubt expressed in almost limitless design in Scripture, one biblical account presents a most memorable example of the fellowship of His suffering. See if you have ever been there.

As mentioned, the resurrection of Jesus ushered in a new relationship with God. While Jesus made multiple references to "Our Father," or "your father," the term "father" can be a term of disappointment for many. Some associate the word "father" with aloofness, rejection, or someone whom they could never satisfy—all based on the negative experiences many have had with their earthly fathers. This is neither God's design nor the norm. Still, this remains the only perception of "father" some know. To indicate a more personal relationship Paul used a word that goes beyond the concept of "father," be that good or bad, by using the word Abba. Abba has an onomatopoeia quality about it, that is, the word consists of a sound that describes itself, such as "buzz" or "meow." Abba was the Aramaic equivalent of "Da Da," "Papa," or "Daddy," and would be one of the first names a toddler would be able to verbalize. Many first time grandparents have the name they want to be called by their grandchild already selected, only to find whatever name the first grandchild speaks becomes their name. Abba would be such a name. It conveys the love of a father with a young child, the tenderness of climbing into Daddy's lap, warmly loved, welcomed, and received.

Paul twice used Abba to indicate the personal love of God the Father for His own. In Romans 6:1–8:17 Paul discussed the ongoing struggle with sin for many believers. Often, one will be saved only to find some area of life remains a continual battle. In Romans 7:19 Paul wrote about the perplexity many believers experience: "For the good I wish, I do not do; but I practice the very evil that I do not wish." Struggling with an area of sin—which differs from glorying in one's sins with no intention of giving it up—causes many Christians to fear. One could reason, "Perhaps God does not love me anymore. I told God I would never do this sin again, and here I am doing it." While certainly not condoning sin, Paul understood both the battle as well as the depth of God's love through Christ. Instead of being disowned by God, Paul informed his readers in Romans 8:15, "You have not received a spirit of slavery leading to fear again, but you have received a spirit of adoption as sons by which we cry out, 'Abba! Father!'" "Crying out" properly relates to the struggle. This is not a crying out in worship or adoration but a crying out to God in one's misery. The term Paul selected was "Abba"—Papa, Daddy. It is personal and relational. It shows the One who warmly and intimately loves us even in our failures and struggles.

Paul's other use of Abba occurs in Galatians 4:6. The Galatians entertained false teachers who caused them to step away from grace and into the confines of the Law. Paul emphasized that following God is not a system, but a Person. One has a relationship with a living Being, not with an encoded system. Instead of being a slave to the Law and laboring under its weighty (and actually humanly unattainable) commands, the Galatians had already been saved by grace. It amazed Paul that the Galatians would abandon Jesus for legalistic bondage. He showed the Galatians what was already theirs in Christ, and what they would abandon by subjugating themselves back into bondage: "And because you are sons [not slaves] God has sent forth the Spirit of His Son into our hearts, crying 'Abba! Father!'" Here the Holy Spirit, not believers, cried Abba out of love and concern for the Galatians. As with Romans, Paul coupled "crying out" with "Abba," denoting the intensity of the plea.

Only one other example exists of Abba recorded in Scripture. This example also accompanies a crying out. Hours before His arrest Jesus entered the Garden of Gethsemane. Many who read the biblical accounts are aware that the garden existed, but they have never really entered there in spirit. My father often took my brothers and me to Civil War battle-fields. We would see the impeccably manicured fields adorned with flowers and shrubbery. While a particular battle took place there long ago, the present landscape did not reflect the atrocities of war. We could not capture the pathos of combat decades before. In the same way, neither do artists' renditions of Jesus in the Garden of Gethsemane properly depict the horror. The sight of Jesus would have abhorred us. He was not well groomed, a heavenly beam radiating on Him as He comfortably kneeled and placed His folded hands on a rock. If Calvary was the ultimate place where Christ secured victory, Gethsemane was the opening salvo in the salvation drama. Gethsemane was a battleground of indescribable warfare.

Taking again Peter, James, and John, Jesus entered a spiritual battle-ground in a way previously unknown even to Him. Mark 14:33 depicts Jesus as "very distressed and troubled." The word "distressed" can also be translated in the Greek as "to be amazed." The connected inference was the depth and intensity of His battle which caused even Jesus to respond in abject horror, terrified dread. Having emptied Himself of the free use of His divine attributes, the severity of the suffering was greater than even He expected. He was surprised. The other word, "troubled," also loses some-thing in its translation. The Greek word means "to be in anguish, or to be extremely troubled." It is not distresses in general but a deep, despondent distress.

Even the movement of Jesus' body reveals the extent of His fight. Mark 14:35 states that Jesus fell to the ground in prayer. Mark used the imperfect tense that usually designates repeated action: Jesus repeatedly fell to the ground in prayer. His prayer was a prayer of movement, of falling face down in anguish before God, of rising, no doubt pacing about, perhaps outstretching His hands to God, of being consumed with horror again, and falling face down again in prayer. Repeated, nonstop agonizing prayer—active prayer in active battle. Matthew records three different segments of Jesus' prayers. He does not reveal their length; they may have lasted for hours. Luke described the suffering as so intense God saw fit to send an angel to strengthen Him. He further described Jesus as being in "great agony," with His sweat becoming like great drops of blood. No blows hitting Him yet, no whips ripping His flesh, not smitten with a rod at this point—yet such intense agony and anguish resulting from the war within Him, it brought physical harm to His body. We will never fully understand it. As the angel who ministered to Jesus and then stepped away from His battle, we, too, stand only as distant spectators—not participants. It was His and His alone. We simply lack the capacity of comprehending what Gethsemane was like for Him.

Yet, God in His mercy permits some of us to peek in from a different angle as to what Jesus endured. In a unique and massively limited way, we do experientially know in a small degree what it was like for Him.

Mark 14:36 reveals a most startling truth: Jesus prayed, "Abba! Father!" It is the only instance recorded in Scripture where Jesus addressed God the Father by this name. The usual Greek word for "father" is *pater*, occurring over two hundred times in Scripture, such as, "Our Father [*pater*] which art in heaven." It is where we get our word "paternal." In His brokenhearted anguish, however, Jesus cried out "Abba! Papa! Daddy!"—not Pater. It was a cry of a wounded child to His protective and loving Father. It was the frustrated cry to Abba to remove His pain, to take His Cup away from Him, if possible. It was the desperate repeated prayer to Abba when Abba did not immediately answer. When Abba finally answered, Abba said "No." The Cup would not be removed—Jesus must drink all of it. So the Son submitted. Yet, the horror would consume Him to the core of His soul, and He would again fall to the ground, crying out "Abba!" If this had been the exact time of His arrest, no torches would have been necessary to find Jesus. The guards simply had to follow the repeated wails of "Abba! Daddy!" These would have led them directly to the Son.

Paul wrote, "that I may know Him . . . and the fellowship of His sufferings," and we have a better understanding of what that means. If you have ever responded in amazed terror at the depths of the suffering God allows on you, His child, you know to a degree the fellowship of His sufferings. If you have ever prayed in fervent passion, broken heartedly crying out to God for rescue, you know an aspect of the fellowship of His suffering. If you have ever been broken in spirit before God, and later crushed that He did not alleviate your suffering, you know some of the fellowship of His suffering. If the answer you seek from God is anything but what you desire, and yet you submit to His will, even when it means more pain, you know firsthand the fellowship of His suffering. It is not that He knows our suffering—which He knows—it is that we know a little of His. And we marvel—and we worship. We know Him better, not more about Him—and we walk away more and more conformed into His image.

Often, people say they go to church "for the fellowship only." Sunday School classes often name themselves "The *Koinonia* Class"—"The Fellowship Class." There is yet another Fellowship Class available whose doors are always open. However, once you enter you are not so much a visitor as you are an eternal member. You will find Jesus there. And Paul. And a long list of faithful ones to the Lord who, not so much by personal choice, but more so by personal perseverance and faith, know the power of His resurrection and the fellowship of His suffering.

Chapter Six

The Footprints

Most of us have read the brief story entitled "Footprints in the Sand." You can find it on plates, magnetized emblems for refrigerators, and framed on walls. It is a touching depiction of a man in heaven reviewing his life with Jesus. Looking back over his life the man sees two sets of footprints during most of the way. However, during the extremely difficult times only one set of footprints in the sand appears. He interpreted this to mean abandonment by God at these crucial points. The Lord instead informs him the single set of footprints belongs to Jesus as He alone carried the man through the midst of his most severe trials.

The Bible repeatedly presents the same core truth of this brief narrative. God does stick closer than a brother. We have His word He will never leave or forsake us. Nothing can separate us from the love of Christ. Even the cherished line from Psalm 23 reminds us, "Even though I walk through the valley of the shadow of death I fear no evil, for Thou art with me; Thy rod and Thy staff, they comfort me."

While "Footprints in the Sand" is one author's depiction of how Jesus will ultimately reveal His previously undetected care for His own, the Bible contains an account of another set of footprints. Not only are these footprints quite literal, they remain even to this day. We are not merely to know about the footprints, but we as believers are to follow on them. While in some ways similar to "Footprints in the Sand," what this passage of Scripture describes is strikingly different, but foundational to our understanding of suffering.

First Peter contains the account. Much had changed by the time Peter wrote this epistle. The Roman government had grown intensely more hostile to Christians. No longer was Christianity viewed as a harmless quirk of misguided fools. Public and political opinions had shifted. The State considered anyone claiming allegiance to Jesus instead of Caesar as its enemy. Sporadic persecution had erupted—but it would grow much worse. The State would persecute untold thousands, subjecting them to physical and financial hardships. Many were beaten—some would be martyred. They committed the heinous crime of claiming the promise of a greater hope and reward in another world through another king, Jesus. Bleak days awaited many Christians of this time. Several leaders of the early church would also face martyrdom, including the Apostle Paul. Sometime shortly before or after Paul's death, Peter himself would be crucified in accord with the prophecy Jesus spoke concerning him.

From the time Jesus took Peter aside on the beach in John 21 and signified with what manner of death Peter would glorify the Lord, Peter had known his life on earth would end in crucifixion. Perhaps this is why he could sleep so soundly after his arrest by Herod in Acts 12. Herod had previously arrested James, the brother of John, and put him to death with the sword. Having observed how the action pleased the Jews, Herod also arrested Peter, no doubt having the same intention of executing him in like manner. However, since Herod could not crucify anyone—that right reserved only for Rome—and since Jesus showed Peter crucifixion would be the manner of Peter's death, Peter could sleep in relative peace. He knew it was not his time.

Shortly after the writing of First Peter, however, would be his time to die. Peter knows his destiny and does not shrink from it. He is a changed man from the Gospel accounts of him that only present Peter's early years of walking with Jesus. He receives much criticism as one who was headstrong, brash, overconfident, and thought more highly of himself than he should. Part of this is true, but much of it would also be true for most of us as well. Not many of us would fare any better. Would you want the first three years of your life with Jesus recorded in Scripture for all to read? How humiliating it would be if God chose to record in writing for the entire world to read at their leisure, even a fraction of the foolish or sinful things we did or said, let alone the deeper struggles or temptations within our heart.

So when Peter wrote First Peter, he was an older man physically, and a much more mature man in the Christian graces. In Acts 4:13 the rulers and elders of Israel recognized Peter and John as "having been with Jesus." We would have observed the same thing on a much deeper level were we able to converse with Peter. For thirty or so years Peter had walked with Jesus, and the effects radiantly beamed in his life. He had put off childish things; he had become an example of the rock of faith Jesus predicted Peter would become.

One difference in Peter at this point versus the Gospel years is he had become a shepherd, but not merely in response to Jesus' threefold injunction to him to feed His lambs. Peter was now a shepherd from the heart. The suffering Peter endured over the decades produced such a change. He no longer would be among those who argued over who was the greatest apostle. He no longer informed the Lord what will and will not be permissible, or boasted in his allegiance to Him. Peter demonstrated this in the care he exhibited for the flock scattered throughout Pontus, Galatia, Cappadocia, Asia, and Bithynia. Interestingly, much of this region consisted of the area God forbade the Apostle Paul to enter in Acts 16. God had not rejected these people; He sent them Peter instead, all in accord with His precise orchestration.

I often challenge my students to drop down into the world of the different biblical characters and see how they would respond if these were their set of circumstances. If you were Peter, what would you write to Christians scattered throughout Asia Minor who not only had already suffered, but faced the likelihood of significantly increased suffering? The persecution would involve entire families, not merely church leaders. The flocks are fearful; they dread the future. To make matters worse the circumstances of the day would seem to indicate Christianity was defeated and on the brink of annihilation. Most of the original apostles and leaders have already been martyred by this time, and now the mighty power of Rome swings against any Christian. If you are in Peter's position, how do you shepherd a flock who faces such intense suffering? You cannot say, "Well, it's not really that bad,"—it was. Neither could you encourage them by writing, "Just hang in there. Things will get better"—they would not, at least for many of them. What do you write to comfort these beleaguered followers of Jesus? How do you shepherd suffering sheep?

Actually, what I asked the students is a trick question. God does not ask us to write how we would do it. Instead, God the Holy Spirit has incorporated into His eternal Word the truths He desires the church to know. We do not have to invent or be creative—we have to be informed and obedient.

Peter began his first epistle by marking the vast contrast between the temporal and the eternal, both in the physical and spiritual realm. Those who view God as under obligation to give them heaven on earth will not think highly of Peter's approach, but it is what the Holy Spirit inspired Peter to employ. The first twelve verses of First Peter consist of the doctrinal foundations, with the remainder of the book exhortations on how one should live based on those truths. Peter referred to the believers as aliens, that is, as those who really are not at home in this world, and directs their focus to their ultimate home with Jesus. He reminds them of the greatness of the salvation they possess by referring to it in reverse chronological order. He begins with the future because that is where Christians will ultimately realize their hope. In the future there is an imperishable and undefiled inheritance already reserved for them in heaven, a reward of inestimable greater value than the totality of what the world has to offer (1:3-5). Although their present trials are severe—Peter does not deny that, nor should we when we encounter the suffering of others—whatever these saints endure or lose while on earth God will abundantly repay many times over. In fact, the salvation that believers currently possess is of such a magnitude angels earnestly long to examine closely everything related to it (1 Pet. 1:12). This is awe-inspiring. Angels have seen all the world has to offer: power, glory, beauty, riches, fame. Yet our salvation is what intrigues them. To put it differently, if you could converse with an angel, and God would permit, an angel would trade places with you despite your present circumstances— an even swap; no questions asked. You become an angel, and he would become a Christian. But, it would be a totally unfair transaction; the angel would get the surpassingly better end of the deal. Even human laws would not allow such a one-sided hoodwinking. Despite suffering and spiritual weariness, the greatness of the salvation for those who know Jesus is what interests angels, and should occupy the majority of believers' thoughts as well.

Throughout the remainder of the epistle Peter calls the believers to willful submission for the sake of Christ. As with Paul and the Philippians, this does not mean to suffer for the sake of suffering or refer to suffering due to the consequences of our own sin, but rather to suffer for the sake of Jesus. It does not mean what the Roman government and individuals did was right. God would most assuredly hold them accountable for all their sins unless they came to a saving knowledge of the truth. But it did mean to count the cost and then to endure out of one's love for Christ. They should not look for battles to fight or seek martyrdom. Instead, they should be model citizens submitting to every human institution and authority, again with the higher calling of submitting to Jesus Christ as their motivation. Such a mindset extended beyond matters concerning Christians and the government. Slaves were to submit to masters; wives were to submit to husbands. Yet no one was exempt. God's Word called all to display humility to one another unto the glory of Jesus.

Before proceeding, we need to allow what Peter wrote to sink into our minds as well. We read things in Scripture about a particular group and think the requirements refer only to them. Sometimes they do, but especially in the epistles, conduct and attitudes are given for the church body for all time. These were real people with real hardships being told to submit in a most hostile arena for the sake of Christ. Most of us are not by nature of the turn-the-other-cheek mentality. It is as alien to us as Peter said his readers were to this world. I am thankful to live in America where, at this time, the State allows certain religious freedoms. But you will not find much in Scripture about "Christian rights." In fact, what the Bible teaches will not please most of those who call themselves believers in Christ. The Bible admonishes us to lay our rights down for the sake of Jesus—and it goes against our grain to think even momentarily about doing this, let alone to put it into practice.

If you were Peter writing to such a group who was suffering unjustly, the operative question in people's hearts would be the age-old, "Why should I?" The trump card Peter repeatedly plays is simply Jesus. Peter does not debate political issues of the day, the evils of the government, or how God's wrath will fall on those who persecute believers. He does not even limit his counsel to "do it for Jesus," which would have been theologically sufficient, but not sufficient for the inner recesses of a suffering heart. Although contrary to human nature, willful submission might be something these Christians could perform externally. Peter, however, does not merely address their outward behavior. He calls for a willing heart that fully trusts in Jesus. To bring his flock to this point, Peter must take them deeper in their comprehension of the person and work of Jesus Christ. Repeatedly throughout the epistle Peter will answer the "why should I?" with "because Jesus did for you," and did so to a degree we too need to understand.

First Peter 2:21-25 is a prime example of Christ as the forerunner and example of enduring suffering according to God's will:

> *For you have been called for this purpose, since Christ also suffered for you, leaving you an example for you to follow in His steps, who committed no sin, nor was any deceit found in His mouth; and while being reviled, He did not revile in return; while suffering, He uttered no threats, but kept entrusting Himself to Him who judges righteously; and He Himself bore our sins in His body on the cross, that we might die to sin and live to righteousness; for by His wounds you are healed. For you were continually straying like sheep, but now you have returned to the Shepherd and Guardian of your souls.*

In the previous context, Peter instructed slaves to submit to masters, even the unreasonable ones. He did not write this for the benefit of harmonious societal workings, nor for the benefit of the master. If ever a "why should I?" would emerge, it would be for a Christian slave to submit willingly to an unreasonable master, with many masters no doubt being unbelievers. How about you? Would you submit, willingly and from the heart? Probably not, especially not of your own initiative. Such exercised humility requires a higher calling. Peter always pointed to Jesus: He did this for you; you follow His example. No complaint registers long whenever Jesus is in view. "It's not fair. It's not right. I deserve better"—anyone want to argue their case above the one Jesus had? We will not be prone to either, if we continually look to Jesus instead of our circumstances.

Yet embedded in these verses are nuggets of truths often passed over, particularly in First Peter 2:21: "For you have been called for this purpose, since Christ also suffered for you, leaving you an example for you to follow in His steps." Such uncovered truths not only open our eyes to the magnificent person and ministry of Jesus, they also encourage us to follow His lead more closely. We need to dissect this verse to get the full impact of what God's Word says, and then apply it to our lives.

What Peter wrote throughout his epistle would be at odds with much modern theology. He began this section in First Peter 2:21 by informing his readers that not only was God fully aware of their suffering, but rather they "were called for this purpose" as an aspect of their Christian walk. Literally the phrase reads, "for into/unto this you were called." The "this" refers to the patient endurance needed when one suffers wrongly as a Christian. As always Peter reinforced what he wrote by using Jesus as both the example, as well as the basis of motivation. Jesus suffered for you. Actually, though, the suffering of Jesus goes much deeper. Peter employed the Greek word *hyper*, sometimes translated "for," but usually one that has a more precise meaning. *Hyper* is a preposition of substitution, usually meaning "in place of," or "in behalf of." What Peter writes could be translated, "Christ suffered in your behalf." He suffered more than just "for" you; He suffered in place of you. It is one thing to suffer so someone else receives the benefit, such as suffering through hard work for the sake of one's family. It is quite another thing to step in and receive the life-ending punishment due someone else so they would not be afflicted. Yet, this is what Christ did for us, or more consistently, what He did in place of us, taking on Himself the penalty and pain due us for our sins.

The next phrase of First Peter 2:21, "leaving you an example to follow in His steps," also has major implications in our understanding of suffering. For instance, "leaving you" is a present participle from the Greek word that means, "to leave behind." It grammatically connects with the verb part of "Jesus suffered." Peter's use of the present tense indicates whatever Jesus left behind still has consequences for believers today; it has not changed or been removed. So what is it Jesus leaves behind? He leaves us an "example to follow," from the Greek word *hypogrammon*. Greek writers of New Testament times used this word in reference to outlines of a sketch that the artist would later fill in with details. The word also referred to the model of handwriting a student just learning to write would copy. The beginner carefully traced over the letters trying to come as close as possible to the "example" he followed. Over the years, the word also figuratively expressed a model of conduct that one should emulate. Each nuance of the definition fits quite well with Jesus leaving us a *hypogrammon* example to follow. Jesus leaves a primary sketch we are to follow. Then the Master paints in the details of our individual lives with the colors and hues He desires, all manipulated with the precision and care He alone can perform. Paul presented the same concept in Ephesians 2:10 where he described believers as God's "workmanship," a word commonly used in Greek for a work of art. Such may be a glimpse into why suffering varies so greatly among those whom the Lord loves. God has established our *hypogrammon* example, which is mostly the same for anyone who follows Jesus. The coloring of the details by Jesus, however, will never be the same for any two people. After all, God never mass-produces masterpieces of His work.

So far in First Peter 2:21 we have Jesus suffering in place of us (not merely "for" us), and leaving (present tense) a *hypogrammon* example (or specific sketch) for us to walk on. What Peter writes next is crucial. We are "to follow in His steps" the example Jesus leaves. The Greek word Peter used means "to follow after, follow closely," or even "to follow upon." What Peter writes is not a matter of following alongside Jesus. Neither is it a matter of Jesus walking with us bringing us through difficult times in our lives. The Bible calls us to walk upon the example Jesus has currently left behind specifically for us. But, we need to understand what that example is by comparing it to what it is not.

To get the full impact of First Peter 2:21, we need to contrast it with Peter's earlier understanding of Jesus decades before. John 13:31-38 is the account of Jesus' last supper with His disciples. Jesus had just dismissed Judas, setting the betrayal, arrest, "trial," and crucifixion into motion. There would be no turning back now. Jesus was alone with His faithful but perplexed disciples. Only precious little time remained with them together, and what Jesus instructed them in their final hours together was not only vital to them, but also to the Church yet to be born. Jesus began, as was and is still so often the case, by saying something totally unexpected, and something no doubt misunderstood. Jesus said, "Now is the Son of Man glorified, and God glorified in Him; if God is glorified in Him, God will also glorify Him in Himself, and will glorify Him immediately" (John 13:31-32). To the disciples—especially Peter, James, and John—this pronouncement was wonderful news. They would naturally think the immediate glorification would include Jesus reigning as king of Israel, with the twelve sitting on thrones judging the tribes of Israel (Matt. 19:28). They might have even been momentarily giddy with anticipation, but if they were it soon changed.

Jesus continued, but what He announced was not what the disciples anticipated. "Little children, I am with you a little while longer. You shall seek Me, and as I said to the Jews, 'Where I am going, you cannot come,' now I say to you also" (13:33). What Jesus said must have jolted the disciples back to the cruel reality of the present hour. This was not glory with Him; it was separation from Him. This was not reigning; it was rejection. The disciples had walked—both physically and spiritually—with Jesus over three years. They had not abandoned Him. Jesus had promised them rewards, specific rewards. It was not so much that rewards were everything, Jesus was everything: their Leader, their Teacher, their Friend—and as they knew then but would understand more clearly later—the Messiah and King, the Son of the living God. In what must have bordered on an insult, they received the same restrictions that Jesus had placed on His enemies: They cannot go where Jesus is going—and it hurts and disturbs them deeply. If they did not know Him better, a germ seed that Jesus may betray them may have sparked across the concourse of their thoughts.

We need to consider what Jesus told them, especially since it would contradict Peter's personality to let what Jesus said go without further interrogation. Jesus informed the disciples they were unable, *dynamai*, in the Greek, meaning they did not have the power or capability to go where He was going. As before, the word is where we get our modern word dynamite. It was not from a lack of permission the disciples could not accompany Jesus—it was from a lack of personal qualification. To go where Jesus would go was uniquely His. No doubt, to have had company would have lessened His anguish. However, as is true in Revelation 5, in all God's creation no one would be found worthy to walk the road He must walk, to drink the cup He must drink.

Before dismissing Judas, Jesus had washed the disciples' feet. When Jesus then predicted one of the disciples would betray him, Peter motioned to John to ask Jesus who the traitor was. Normally, Peter himself would have asked, but having been mildly but sternly rebuked only moments before by Jesus for interfering with the foot washing, Peter most likely would have hesitated to speak again. Nobody enjoys being rebuked in the presence of others, especially by the One whom Peter greatly loved and sought to serve. Yet, the pronouncement by Jesus that He would not allow them to go with Him was simply too much for Peter to endure in silence. Jesus spoke of separation, the one thing Peter feared more than all else, and it prompted Peter to inquire further. Separation did not fit his perception of glory, and it did not fit his perception of Jesus. Jesus had never before told Peter, "You cannot go where I am going." Instead Jesus repeatedly said,

"Come," to Peter, such as when Jesus walked on water, or when Jesus took only Peter and two others into the room where He restored the life of a little girl. Even more to the point, Jesus had invited Peter to witness the preview kingdom glory at the Transfiguration. God would glorify Jesus immediately, but Peter would not be allowed to be with Jesus because he was not able to come with Him? How could this be? This made absolutely no sense to Peter, and he had to discover the reason for the change in plans.

Jesus continued instructing the disciples concerning the love they would manifest to the world as strong proof of their discipleship, but Peter's mind had already cut off by this time. Loving others had no place in his current thoughts. Peter asked two questions, the first for clarification, the second being the genuine question of his heart. "Lord, where are You going?" Actually, Jesus leads Peter to ask the real issue of his heart by the way He answered him. "Where I go, you (singular, not plural)—you—Peter—not all of you, the disciples—cannot follow Me now, but you shall follow later (John 13:36). Such a prohibition exposed Peter's primary concern. "Lord, why can I not follow you right now?" Peter does not say, "Why can we not follow you?" because his heart is not concerned with "we," it is concerned with him. He wants to know why he cannot come with Jesus. He could reason, "I can understand why you would not allow the others to follow, but it is I—Peter! I've always been on the inside. I'm the chief disciple, part of the inner circle. You've never stopped me before. You called me to be with You, not away from You, and that is what I intend to do for the rest of my life." But, if such was his thought Peter did not grasp the words of Jesus. Again, what Jesus forbade was not a prohibition of permission but rather a statement of Peter not having the power or capability at this point to go where Jesus would.

To correct further what Peter considered was Jesus' erroneous evaluation of his level of commitment and loyalty, Peter promised the Lord, "I will lay down my life for you." We need to note the full implication of what Peter proposed: "I will lay down my life for [*hyper*] you." Literally what Peter said was, "The life of mine in place of yours I will lay down." Peter does not say, "I will die with you," as Thomas said in John 11:16. Neither does Peter say, "I will die for you or because of you," as is written about the souls of those in Revelation 6:9 who had been slain "because of the testimony they had maintained." Peter does not boast He will lay down His life with Christ alongside Him, the two of them together. He boasts he will lay down his life so Jesus would not have to. This is actually the same proposal Peter rebuked Jesus with in Matthew 16:22 when he reproved Jesus, saying, "God forbid it, Lord! This shall never happen to You," in response to the news of Jesus' approaching death. Different wording—same issue: Peter still attempted to redeem Jesus from His God-ordained mission.

Jesus strongly rebuked Peter in Matthew 16. Perhaps due to the sympathy of the Good Shepherd knowing what the next few days would entail for Peter, or perhaps due only to lack of time, Jesus responded differently this time—and it must have cut Peter to his core. Jesus simply set forth the sheer irrationality of Peter's boast by restating virtually word for word Peter's statement, but as a question. Jesus asked, literally, in John 13:38, "The life of yours in place of Mine, you will lay down?" It is just as well Scripture does not record the look Jesus gave Peter as He spoke these words, for no writer could do it justice. Jesus—only steps away from the agony of Gethsemane, only hours away from the humiliation and the torture, who will by daybreak be nailed to the cross, who will endure the totality of satanic assault thrown against Him, and who will for the first time in eternity have God the Father turn away from Him, the depth of torture reserved only for One so capable—looked at His "replacement." This is not a satanic temptation to have another step in and take His place. This is merely the next step in the suffering of Jesus, perhaps even more painful than the betrayal by Judas. Peter offers Jesus his meager grain of sand, which in reality is not even his at all, in place of the weight of Mount Hermon. It is human nature to suffer more when others do not properly understand the depths which one's suffering reaches. Jesus knew His depth, and to have it equated with the misguided offer of Peter must have driven the pain deeper.

Jesus might have said more if matters were not so pressing. Yet by merely repeating Peter's words so much could be deduced: "Your life in behalf of Mine you will give? Peter, I am the Good Shepherd who lays down His life for [*hyper*] the sheep, not you. You are trying to step in and take the place rightfully given to Me by God the Father. Peter, if you die in place of Me, by the world's standard, it may be noble or heroic; it may even become the source of fables handed down from generation to generation. To lay down your life may be something of which you would take pride in and possibly may even motivate others to follow your example. But, it will not be accepted by the Father as an atoning sacrifice. It will not be the basis for the forgiveness of your sins—let alone for those of anyone else. At one of my first encounters with you, you told me, 'Depart from me for I am a sinful man.' Who will pay for your own sins, sinful man? Can you undo even one of the myriad of transgressions you yourself have committed? No, your sins permanently disqualify you. You cannot be, or ever could become, the Unblemished Lamb. No, Peter, I will lay down My life in behalf of you—and in place of any sheep that will ever be born. Sin has stained your life. I and I alone am able. Your 'help' to Me at this point is only an impediment. In fact, to show you the vastness between My capacity and your utter incapacity, three times before daybreak you shall deny that you even know I exist."

Scripture records nothing else Peter spoke until Jesus and the disciples reached the Garden. Not fully understanding what Jesus said was painful enough, but having Jesus predict Peter would deny Him—spoken in the full hearing of the other disciples—placed restraints on any further questioning by Peter. His only option at that point was to listen and to try to absorb. Still his mind churned. What Jesus does is painful; what Peter cannot do is even more so. It wounds Peter's pride that Jesus does not permit him to go wherever He was going. It pains him that Jesus esteems Peter so lightly that He would think Peter would deny Him. Since Jesus spoke of a pending separation, Peter probably wondered, "I wonder when He will leave us?" when in reality the reverse would be true. The Father would smite the Shepherd, and the sheep would flee. Peter, in a last attempt of bravery by standing near to where the Sanhedrin initially tried Jesus, would fulfill Jesus' prophecy by three times denying that he even knew Jesus, let alone loved Him. No promise of laying down his life in place of His then. In one of the most stabbing verses of all Scripture, Luke 22:61 records that Jesus turned and looked at Peter in the midst of Peter's final denial. Could artists accurately record the pathos of such a look as the Good Shepherd turns His face to His stumbling sheep? The text says Peter went out and wept bitterly. He had no recourse; the tearing away of one's heart always results in the deep weeping of the soul.

The look of Jesus is not for Peter alone. It meets us at our denials of Jesus as well. It meets us when we are consumed by suffering and the unfairness of the world and, whether by thought or by words, rebuke Him for not properly intervening as we deem He should. The look of Jesus meets us when we proudly state we will follow Him wherever He leads, even unto death, and then grumble when the direction goes in the opposite way we expected. If you look only at your suffering, you cannot look on the face of Jesus; but the reverse is true as well. If you look intently at Jesus, your own suffering does not necessarily go away, but it will become secondary. When you contemplate His suffering for us—or rather in place of us—it makes our suffering more bearable. Instead of concluding, "He does not know what I am going through," you have the solid assurance He does know and, in fact, knows better than we do in our limited capabilities can. Understanding the suffering of Jesus in even a little more depth changes our perspective, making us even worshipful in the midst our own suffering. To put it as Paul did, instead of Jesus knowing about our suffering, we attain a certain amount of the fellowship of His suffering—and we are transformed from the inside out, as God wields this tool as a means of making us more Christ-like.

Let us return to First Peter 2:21 to tie this together. Remember over thirty years have passed since the events of John 13. Peter has learned by experience. The events of that one night decades before changed Peter's life for eternity. Now he is older; now he teaches others what he himself received from the Lord. Notice how similar and how different First Peter 2:21 is from Peter's boast in John 13: For you have been called for this purpose, since Christ also suffered for [hyper] you (not only for you but in place of you, going where you could not go), leaving an (present tense) example for you to follow in His steps." Peter even employed the same Greek word "follow" Jesus used in telling Peter, "Where I am going you cannot follow me now, but shall follow me later." Peter learned—oh, how Peter had learned. Jesus suffered in place of [hyper] us, not us for Him. The suffering that afflicts us may be because of our faith in Him, or even granted by Him, but never will it be in place of Him or His suffering. Simply put, unless Jesus suffered in place of [hyper] us, there would be no "us"—there would only be the Godhead and holy angels. Every other created being would stand as Their defiled antagonists. We must follow on His path, not concoct our own. We are to follow, not to lead. The emphasis is on what He did, not what we do, and it will remain that way throughout the remainder of eternity.

But, there is another point of consideration in First Peter 2:21 we need to explore. We are to follow upon "His steps" or literally, "in the footprints of Him." In the plural the word means a line of footprints, such as when a hunter follows his game. "Footprints" is a literal term, not a figurative one. A difference exists between following in someone's footprints versus following in someone's footsteps. "To follow in someone's footsteps," means to emulate or aspire to some aspect of that person's life. "Are you going to follow in your father's footsteps?" Literal footprints, however, give a different emphasis. Not only are these "footprints in general" but the footprints of Jesus.

So the expanded thought of what Peter wrote is, "For you have been called for this very purpose," namely, to respond in the way Jesus did to the suffering so undeservedly given to Him, by faith and patience, trusting God in the midst of it. "Since Christ suffered [*hyper*] in your place;" suffered in the realm you would not because you could not. "Leaving you"—present tense, not past tense; whatever He left is still there, it has not been removed—a *hypogrammon* example or sketch for you to follow in His footprints. If His footprints remain behind, then He had to walk there first. He had to lead the way. He had to establish a trail that no one ever walked before, but now one that never needs establishing again.

A pertinent question is, "But where do the footprints of Jesus go? If I follow them, where will they lead?" Perhaps the first inclination would be to assume they go up to heaven and into God's very presence. But, this is not the immediate place they go. The last footsteps Jesus took on this earth before His death were to His cross. He was carried to the tomb and placed there. He ascended to heaven—He did not walk. The last steps Jesus took in His pre-resurrection ministry were in walking as the sacrifice in our place, not only so that we would not have to walk there, but even more to the point because we could not. In this case, we do not walk alongside Him—He walked there alone. No one went with Him; nobody could. He was abandoned, deserted, forsaken, and betrayed for you and for me.

Another aspect of this passage is so childishly simple, we may overlook it. You do not "follow upon" footprints by standing still. You must move forward. This entails more than merely knowledge about Jesus; it is experiential knowledge gained in the walk itself. Also, a difference remains between following the line of footprints to the end versus following merely a few steps. "I'll go with you a little while, but if things don't work out as I planned, then you go on without me." Such an attitude became evident for the first time in John 6:66-69 where many would no longer walk with Jesus. To Peter's credit, that answer he got right. In response to Jesus' question if they, too, wanted to leave, Peter answered his most logical reply recorded in Scripture. "Lord, to whom shall we go? You have words of eternal life." And He still does.

You will only walk upon the footprints of Jesus; you never out-walk them. No matter where you are, or what you will go through, He will have walked an infinitely more intense road in your place. You will still find His footprints ahead of your own.

"But there are so many footprints and paths out there for people to follow. How will I know which ones are His footprints?"

You will recognize the footprints of Jesus; they are the only ones left when all the others stop. You will recognize His footprints; they are the ones stained with blood, as He heads for our cross. You will recognize the footprints of Jesus; they are the ones that have your name written all over them.

Chapter Seven

The Surprise

My children are of such an age that I can bring my entire household into a state of frenzy by announcing, "I have a surprise for you." Immediately their young minds attempt to discover what the surprise might be. Is it big? Is it small? Does it bark? Is it here now, or do we have to wait? They usually do not know what the surprise is, but they reason since it comes from me, it must be good.

Peter wrote to the beleaguered churches of Asia Minor, "Do not be surprised," or literally, "stop being surprised,"using a present tense; their existing state was already one of surprise. Peter knew of the fiery ordeals that came upon them for their testing but instructed the believers not to consider their situation strange (1 Peter 4:12). Yet not to be surprised was most demanding for these believers. Their trials and suffering did not harmonize with their understanding of God or with their perception of salvation. As we have seen, the suffering these churches endured was extremely intense and would grow worse. Some members would become martyrs for their faith. Some would suffer physically, others financially, all because they trusted Jesus and walked in obedience to Him. They, as we, no doubt knew numerous references in Scripture that speak of God's love and protection, plus multiple examples where God intervened and saved those in peril from certain death or destruction.

Sometimes, however, God chooses not to intervene when we ask Him, or at least intervene in the way we expect. As was true with the first century Christians, and with countless believers throughout history, we do not understand. We too are surprised. In fact, some verses only add to our confusion because they claim for us blessings that do not seem to be true, or at least true for us. For example, in the same epistle where he addressed the fiery ordeals that afflicted the believers, Peter also comforted his flock by telling them they were currently "protected by the power of God" (1 Peter 1:5). The believers no doubt had a difficult time in appropriating such a promise in the midst of their suffering. If God currently protected them, why were they suffering so intensely? Maybe God's protection was not what they thought it was, or maybe it had some holes in it. Yet this still did not match what they understood to be true about God's might and power, especially what they knew about His active love for them. They had good reason to be surprised, and Peter did not rebuke them for it. What Peter did was take them deeper into the mind of God so they could consider their suffering from God's perspective. While surprised at the degree of suffering they presently faced, they would be equally surprised at Peter's counsel to them.

One of the main reasons for the surprise of these churches was that they were collectively walking in obedience to God. They needed no rebuke for lack of faith or some known sin in their midst. Peter knew this, and lovingly addressed his readers as "obedient children" (1:14), who had been born again unto God (1:3, 23). While this is reassuring, it further adds to our confusion regarding suffering. Since Scripture also describes us as "children of God," it is quite natural to expect God to treat us in the same manner we would our own children. We understand in theory that God would not purposefully cause a catastrophe on His faithful children any more than we would our own. God is a God who loves, and bringing suffering on one in a love relationship with Him makes no sense to us. However, the Bible teaches us God often does not work in the manner we would, His thoughts and ways not being ours. Consideration of other factors, particularly those concerning our adversary the Devil, is in order. Satan most assuredly will cause devastating attacks on the children of God whenever he can. For instance, Job 1–2 indicates Satan, not God, murdered Job's children and caused Job intense physical and emotional pain. Yet in the midst of his suffering Job called out against God, not Satan, since Job was ignorant of Satan's role in his loss. However, while the account in Job reveals satanic powers may be operative in ways we are not aware, it still leaves us with an unsettling question. What we in our human limitations fail to understand is that God had the power and capability to stop Satan from such an attack. Yet for Job, and perhaps in other cases as well, God chose not to restrain him. Why would God purposefully allow Satan to attack and plunder one whom He loved? Again, it does not match our understanding of God nor His promise to protect His own. We would not allow such an attack on our own children, especially if we had the power to keep it from occurring, and we cannot understand why God would permit it on His children.

We are far beyond being surprised. We are back to being perplexed.

We claim verses of deliverance and protection, and still evil reigns. We pray for rescue, and instead the suffering often intensifies. We seek God and His answers, and yet answers do not come, at least not in the form of deliverance we perceive to be the solution. We suffer, and God does not ease the suffering. The intensity and depth of suffering surprises us. How could God do this to us? Even if God did not cause this ordeal, why would He not keep us from it when He had the power and authority to do so? Perhaps this is one of the most discouraging aspects of the surprise: We are surprised at the longevity of suffering. Often, we think our suffering has ended, only to be surprised at another round just beginning, and this bout often even more intense than before. How long must I suffer? How long must I suffer alone? The experiential answers we receive baffle us. It also surprises us when the immediate deliverance does not come.

Many details regarding suffering mystify us. For instance, one of the most startling truths in Job's story is God initiated Job's testing by asking Satan, "Have you considered My servant Job? For there is no one like him on the earth, fearing God and turning away from evil" (1:8). Satan's responding accusation was one God forces us to address as well: "Does Job fear God for nothing?" Satan's argument was Job—and we—serve God for what we receive from God, not for who God is. Remove the blessings you have given him, Satan accused, and Job would curse God to His face. It is an accusation that chills us to our innermost being, if we honestly consider the totality of what such a satanic attack would entail in our lives. We also know if Satan's accusation is true, and here it appears to be, God had placed a hedge of protection around Job that hindered Satan from attacking. We expect Satan would ask for the removal of the protective hedge, but not that God would grant Satan's request. Here is another example of our ways and understanding being totally at odds with God's. If it were in our power to do so, we would never allow the removal of the protective hedge from our children so Satan, or anyone else, could devastate them. Nonetheless

God allowed such an attack. God limited Satan so he could not murder Job, but all else Job had was open to Satan's carnage: his children, his health, his possessions, his status in the community, his peace and well-being—almost every element by which we define our life and enjoyment. Still one of the deepest wounds in this scenario was God purposefully hiding His presence in the midst of Job's agony, despite Job repeatedly calling out to Him. If you were God, would you have done the same thing to one who trusted You? Would you treat your faithful child in such a way? Is this Job's "reward" for being the most upright of anyone who lived on earth at that time? We comprehend that Satan will attack wherever and whenever he can but not that God permits the attack. It makes no sense to us. It surprises us that God would do such a thing to Job. We are surprised when God does not answer Job when Job calls out to Him. We are even more surprised when similar sufferings encompass us. The germ seed of doubt inferring it is sinful for God to fail to protect and purposefully allow intense suffering on those who follow Him may take root in our minds.

We will never have the complete answers to such unanswerable questions during our lifetime. God does not necessarily promise us full disclosure, but, then again, neither did He leave us in complete spiritual ignorance. For instance, observing the life of Job gives us a glimpse into one of the reasons faithful followers of God suffer. A spiritual warfare rages that is invisible to human cognizance, with Satan being the antagonist against God and His people, which includes us. We are a little more enlightened than Job, but not much. Since we also cannot see all the factors involved, we often are not certain about the origin or purpose of our suffering, especially when we are in the midst of it. No spiritual barometer exists which indicates this suffering is due to satanic influence, but this one is not. As was true for Job, circumstances limit us to only observing the symptoms of suffering and making our own limited deductions, which most likely will not be any more accurate than were those of Job. Graciously, God has chosen to reveal more information in Scripture about the surprise of suffering He permits on His own. We have a better understanding of the particulars of suffering—and if believed and appropriated, a much better hope. We will find much of this in First Peter. As always, virtually everything Peter wrote years later in his epistles originates from his education during the earthly ministry of Jesus.

When Peter wrote of the "testing" endured by his readers in First Peter 4:12, he employed one of two Greek words generally translated "trials" or "testings." Suffering may accompany both words. Yet, the difference between the two words is striking regarding the origins and intentions of the trials. In their simplest terms, *peirasmos* is a testing looking for one to fail while *dokimos* is a testing to show the value or quality of the thing tested. While there are a few exceptions, the first word has a bad connotation; the second has primarily a good one. An example of *peirasmos* being used without an evil intent occurs in the account of the feeding of the five thousand, when Jesus asked Philip "Where are we going to buy bread, that these may eat?" John 6:6 states, "And this He was saying to test him [*peirasmos*]; for He Himself knew what He was intending to do." In this case, Jesus intended for Philip to fail this test. Jesus wanted Philip to conclude that he and the others alone did not have sufficient resources, but Jesus did. However, this good use of *peirasmos* is an exception. The overwhelming examples in the New Testament have this word for a testing to fail, a severe temptation, or a trial quite often linked with evil connotations. Merely realizing which word is used in strategic Scripture passages gives a starting point for understanding the origin of some of our trials.

For instance, *peirasmos* occurs twelve times in the Synoptic Gospels for the temptations or testings encountered by Jesus. The agents for these testings were either Satan or the earthly opponents of Jesus. Such testings were attempts at causing failure and ruin, and obviously they did not originate from God. People sometimes perceive Jesus to have been on "automatic pilot" spiritually, that is, responding to temptation was easy for Him. Actually, Hebrews 2:18 indicates just the opposite: "For since He Himself was tempted [a verb form of *peirasmos*] in that which He has suffered, He is able to come to the aid of those who are tempted" [*peirasmos*]. Likewise, Hebrews 4:15 states, "For we do not have a high priest who cannot sympathize with our weaknesses, but one who has been tempted [*peirasmos*] in all things as we are, yet without sin." If you were God, how would you go about "building" a Messiah? One way God chose was to allow Jesus to suffer through His temptations the totality of what Satan had to afflict, and yet remain sinless. Instead of thinking, "Jesus does not know how bad it is," in reality He does know how bad it is and then some, since He experienced the full weight of satanic testing. On the other hand, God actively protects us. First Corinthians 10:13 states, "No temptation [*peirasmos*] has overtaken you but such as is common to man; and God will not allow you to be tempted [*peirasmos*] beyond what you are able, but with the temptation [*peirasmos*] will provide the way of escape also, that you may be able to endure it." As bad as our *peirasmos* trials may be, God knows how much each one of us individually can endure, and He will not permit it to reach beyond that point. However, God placed no such restriction with Jesus, and Satan rendered his greatest testing for our Savior. Suffering was a necessary aspect of preparing Jesus to be our High Priest. Hebrews 5:8 informs us, "Even though He was a Son, He learned obedience through the things He suffered," and much of His suffering was a result of the *peirasmos* trials He encountered.

Man has questioned the origin of evil and why the righteous suffer since the beginning of time. God reveals in Scripture glimpses into the nature and reason for some of our suffering, such as seen in the use of *peirasmos*. Satan hates God and those aligned with Him. If you are in God's fold, you have—present tense, continuing action—an enemy. As Peter wrote, Satan actively "prowls around seeking someone to devour" (1 Pet. 5:8). Peter's next verse demonstrates the resulting sufferings of believers occurring all over the world, along with the inference to the satanic source for the suffering: "But resist him, firm in your faith, knowing that the same experiences of suffering are being accomplished by your brethren who are in the world" (5:9). We must understand the warfare has not subsided any since Peter wrote; Satan still inflicts sufferings on God's children throughout the world. While Satan cannot devour someone in the sense of taking away their position in Christ, these verses indicate a major emphasis of his attack is on those saved (why should Satan waste his effort with those who are not walking with the Lord?), and suffering is one of the byproducts of his attack. As happened with Job, sometimes we wrongly state the origin of suffering, automatically assuming God struck and afflicted us, when the truth is Satan may be the source. James 1:13 makes it clear while God may allow and even use a trial for His objectives, He Himself is not the origin of evil: "Let no one say when He is tempted, 'I am tempted by God,' for God cannot be tempted by evil, and He Himself does not tempt anyone." Four times in this one verse James employed a form of *peirasmos* to indicate God is not the source of such temptations that lead to sin, failure, or falling away from Him.

Scripture repeatedly tells, however, of one who always tempts with a view toward failure and fall. For instance, Matthew 4:3 describes Satan as "the tempter," using a form of *peirasmos* in giving a suitable description of both his character and activity. Through his close association with Jesus, Peter knew such satanic attacks were not reserved for only the spiritually mature or those who feel as though they are ready to meet them. When one initially hears the Gospel, Satan begins his sinister testings. In the Parable of the Sower in Luke 8:13, Jesus described the rocky soil as "those who, when they hear, receive the word with joy; and these have no firm root; they believe for a while, and in time of temptation [*peirasmos*] fall away." As indicated in First Peter 5:8, Satan "prowls about like a roaring lion, seeking someone to devour." Peter took the prowling of the adversary most seriously. Paul did, too, and listed prayer as one of the major components of the spiritual armor God has provided the believer (Eph. 6:18). Peter would "amen" this wholeheartedly. He had heard Jesus pray in the Disciple's Prayer "and do not lead us into temptation [*peirasmos*], but deliver us from evil," or literally, "from the evil one" (Matt. 6:13). Believers should be watchful in prayer so the *peirasmos* types of temptations do not overcome them. While it is impossible to avoid all trials, you can respond properly to them and actually affect their outcome.

One reason one cannot avoid such trials is that God, in His sovereign design and for reasons unknown to us, sometimes allows Satan to inflict the *peirasmos* testing on the ones He loves. We saw this with Job; it was also true with Jesus. In Matthew 4:1 the Holy Spirit led Jesus into the wilderness for Satan to tempt Jesus. As expected Matthew employs a form of *peirasmos* to describe Satan's testing of Jesus. Yet Jesus withstood what Adam had not and passed the test that the nation of Israel continually failed. While the temptations in the wilderness, Gethsemane, and Calvary were the most severe *peirasmos* tests inflicted on Jesus, Luke 22:28 discloses Jesus was the subject of satanic temptation throughout His entire life, especially the years of His earthly ministry. On the night of the Last Supper Jesus addressed His disciples as "those who have stood by Me in My trials" [*peirasmos*] (plural). One mistake, one sinful response, one misuse of His power, one following through on a lustful thought, one selfish act, one wrong thing said—any inappropriate response to a *peirasmos* testing, and our Lamb would become blemished, our Shepherd soiled, our Savior disqualified. Gethsemane and Calvary are magnificent demonstrations of the love and majesty of Jesus so beyond our human understanding that we could more easily perceive the full scope of God's creation than we could the depths of

His love displayed there. But for Jesus to live every day of His life in sinless perfection; to receive the totality of satanic assault and temptation, yet never stumble or trip; to press on in obedience to God's leading, even when the leading resulted in severe suffering, and the sufferings eventually lead to death—we are speechless in awe, or at least should be. When the *peirasmos* onslaughts pulverize us and we suffer, we realize to a much clearer degree our own limitations, weaknesses, and the need for God's engulfing grace. We have a better understanding of the strength of Jesus, realizing how quickly we fall and stumble with only a billionth of what He endured. If you follow God's design, suffering will make you more appreciative and worshipful of the Savior and intimately closer to Him. We realize only limited suffering in our lives often causes us to respond poorly, recognizing our total ineptitude to comprehend the extent of His suffering in our behalf, and yet remain without sin. Not only could we not endure His testings, we cannot even begin to perceive their magnitude.

When Peter wrote his two epistles, he greatly understood trials and testing that lead to suffering to a much greater degree than he did during the Gospel accounts. He also had a much greater respect for their magnitude. As before, crisis situations occurred in Peter's life that changed him forever, particularly events during the last few days before the crucifixion of Jesus. On the night of His betrayal Jesus approached Peter and warned him what would transpire in the upcoming moments, not at some time far removed in the distant future (Luke 22:31). "Simon, Simon"—Jesus employed Peter's pre-faith name. Peter would be no "rock" of faith tonight; he would sink like a rock—"behold"—pay attention! "Satan has demanded permission to sift you like wheat." Peter, being raised as a Jew, plus having been taught personally by Jesus for over three years, should have recognized the similarity between Satan's request to sift Peter and his previous request concerning Job. Satan received divine permission to afflict Job, and now he could sift Peter in similar manner. Job was not forewarned; Peter was, but he underestimated both the severity of the attack and the hatred of the attacker. He was about to learn these firsthand.

The account of Luke 22:31 is the parallel account of John 13:31-38, where Jesus informed Peter and the others they were not permitted to follow Him then, but they would follow later. It is where Peter offered his life in place of the life of Jesus. Luke gives us additional insight into Peter's thoughts and reasoning. Peter listened to Jesus, but he did not really hear what He said. The events of the past week swirled over and through him and the other disciples with such speed they were incapable of sifting through them all. They did not have their bearings any more than one caught in a whirlpool, and the seeming contradictions of what they heard and saw only added to their confusion. The masses adored Jesus at the Triumphal Entry, and yet Jesus repeatedly informed the disciples of His pending death. He spoke of His glory now to be revealed, with His faithful apostles ruling with Him, but He also predicted His rejection, scourging, and crucifixion. He spoke with them as friends, and yet predicted one would betray Him. All the disciples, perhaps except Peter, suppressed the current of fright that they themselves might be the one of whom Jesus spoke. Partly because of their own fear, they did not identify Judas as the traitor when Jesus dismissed him from their presence.

Alone with the Twelve minus one, Jesus again reinforced what He had taught before. "And you are those who have stood by Me in My trials," Jesus explained in Luke 22:28, which must have been reassuring since He had just previously announced one would betray Him. Perhaps at that point the eleven could have reasoned the traitor was Judas, but neither time nor sorrow permitted such deductions one makes in leisure. "And just as My Father has granted Me a kingdom, I grant you that you may eat and drink at My table in My kingdom, and you will sit on thrones judging the twelve tribes of Israel." Days earlier Jesus had promised the same thing as He and His disciples approached Jerusalem, but in the present context, as seen in John 13:31-32, He spoke of His impending glorification: "Now is the Son of Man glorified, and God is glorified in Him; if God is glorified in Him, God will also glorify Him in Himself, and will glorify Him immediately." However, in the midst of the promised blessings and the disciples' revelries concerning the imminent kingdom glory and their rewards came Jesus' shocking prohibition against the disciples following Him now. A kingdom, yet trials, they could understand. Glory, yet separation, they could not—especially Peter.

It is at this point Luke records Jesus' emphatic warning to Peter concerning the horrendous trial Peter would face in the next few hours. In fact, Jesus indicated what had already been granted to the adversary. Satan had obtained permission to sift Peter like wheat, not that he sought permission or was even in the process of asking. Satan had already asked, and God granted his petition. This may offer some insight into the Devil's methodology of attack. We would think Satan would focus his attack that night on Jesus, which no doubt he did, that being Satan's hour. Yet, here the evil one selected one of the Shepherd's own, and later the Shepherd's entire flock, to afflict with a *peirasmos* temptation. Perhaps realizing the futility of making Christ stumble in a face-to-face confrontation Satan turned to one loved of Christ. Perhaps it was a ploy to have the loving Shepherd focus on one of His lambs instead of on His own pending agony, and then be ill-prepared for the cup He must drink, having no comparison in eternity equal to it. It is speculative, and we will never know the answer this side of heaven. But what is evident is Jesus, having loved them unto the end, prayed for Peter when Jesus Himself would suffer immeasurably more and be tempted far beyond the limitations of Peter. Jesus prayed for Peter although Peter deemed it unnecessary for Jesus to waste His time doing so. Satan made his request before God—but so did Jesus. God heard and answered both.

At this point, Peter did not actually believe Jesus. He believed in Him, knowing more certain than ever that Jesus was the Christ, the Son of the Living God, but Peter did not believe what Jesus told him. The prayer of the divine Jesus to the divine Father was that Peter's faith may not fail—not that Peter himself would not fail—and that Peter would turn again, and strengthen his brothers (Luke 22:32). Jesus knew what would transpire. He spoke not so much a prophecy as He did a pronouncement of what was taking place that very moment, yet Peter could not conceive it was true. In Luke 22:33 Peter began his response to Jesus' warning with *de*, usually translated "but," and used as a mild rebuttal against what had been spoken. In his early walk with the Lord, Peter generally responded to the Lord's pronouncements with the disagreeing "but," which in reality equates to, "I do not fully or even partially agree with what You have just said," or, the all-encompassing, "It does not make sense to me, so therefore, it must not be true." But it was true. Peter would be sifted like wheat; he, but not his faith, would fail. He eventually would turn again and strengthen his brothers. Peter would do so in the upcoming days after the crucifixion of Jesus, and he would continue to do so the remainder of his life. Even his instruction in his two epistles decades later is a partial fulfillment of the prayer Jesus prayed that night.

But, this night would be a time of darkness and defeat, a time foreknown by the Lord, a lesson about to mark Peter for a lifetime. Peter wrote from personal experience in First Peter 5:5, "God is opposed to the proud, but gives grace to the humble," and Peter was about to be humbled.

If Jesus expanded His warning to Peter, it would be something like, "Simon, Simon—and I have not called you by this name for months. You were Simon when I first met you. You shall be called Peter, the Rock, and at times you have been, but events tonight will overcome you that will reveal to you the Simon you remain at your core. You have walked with Me, learned from Me, and were even empowered by Me to do miracles, but you have also been an easy prey for Satan, as you still are tonight. You once tried to hinder me from the cross, and I had to rebuke you. Not only did you not stand then, you did not even recognize the attack for what it was—and tonight will be exceedingly worse for you. Satan has taken it upon himself to ask permission from God the Father, and you are one of the main objects of his hate-filled desire. Satan has received permission to sift you in much the same way one sifts wheat. It is a painful sifting that will reduce and remove the chaff within you, and there is always anguish whenever any portion of you is removed. You will come out with some of you missing; you will come out scarred for life. Only one time earlier had it been revealed by the Father that Satan had been granted permission to act out his inner hatred, and that was with Job. You know what happened then. You are moments away from entering the same arena that Job unwittingly entered. He did not know in what realm he was, but you are forewarned. Your only hope is My prayer for you and your faith in Me, and even then you will be sifted to your soul—and you will fail."

If we were in Peter's situation, knowing what would transpire, would we believe Jesus? I think we would, at least then. Would we not cling to Jesus? Would not the thought of pending attack so greatly terrify us we would try our best to be with Him, beside Him? We sometimes disparage Peter for his stubbornness in not heeding the words of the Lord, but are we really any different? Not only can we view Job's life, we can also view Peter's, and yet we also have difficulty believing Jesus and His word. We conclude we are alone when we suffer, and yet the Bible tells us nothing can separate us from the love of God in Christ. We know the outcome of their suffering and see how God used it, and even recognize Satan's hand in it, and yet we cannot bring ourselves to rejoice in the midst of our sharing of the sufferings of Christ. We chide Peter for deeming himself stronger than he was, and yet we silently or verbally perceive ourselves as seasoned veterans of walking with Jesus, ready and able to stand firm against attacks the magnitude of which we have no knowledge. Through God's grace we might have survived trials in the past and seen God intervene, but sifting is a different hazard, wrought under distinct conditions, played under unique rules. Only moments later in Gethsemane Jesus instructed His disciples, "Pray that you may not enter into temptation" [*peirasmos*]. But, they did not pray and *peirasmos* temptation came upon them—especially Peter. It was a testing they would remember the rest of their lives.

While Peter did not fully understand the warning by Jesus, Peter's initial response actually shows his deep faith in Jesus. In Luke 22:33 Peter answered, "Lord, with You [and the 'with You' begins Peter's reply in the Greek, being positioned there for emphasis] I am ready to go both to prison and to death!" Therein is the key. Peter was more accurate than people give him credit. His was not a boast but rather a concluded reality. With Jesus, Peter could do the impossible and exhibit the supernatural courage and strength of Jesus, such as walking on water with Him. However, John 13 informs us it was in this context Jesus had just announced His pending separation from the disciples, and of course, this included separation from Peter. With Jesus, Peter would draw his sword before the hundreds sent to arrest Jesus. Without Jesus, Peter would reel from the simple question of a teenage handmaiden. With Jesus, Peter had confidence. Without Jesus, Peter had a naive self-confidence that simply hastened his downfall. With Jesus, Peter was Peter; without Him, Peter was Simon. As the events of the night unfolded, the sifting occurred. Peter underwent the agony of the chaff being removed. The man failed—but not the man's faith. Simon died, but Peter was born, and with his birth the accompanying pains of childbirth.

So much is embedded in this one brief scenario from which we can observe and learn, but so much more remains beyond our grasp. As noted earlier, we cannot fathom the look Jesus gave Peter in the midst of Peter's profane denials of even knowing Jesus, let alone being closely associated with Him. But there is another look we cannot perceive. How could God bring Himself to look at Satan as Satan made his request before Him, a request resulting in the collapse of faithful follower Peter, and even more so, in the torturous death of His own Son? The abject audacity of Satan to approach the exalted Almighty God and request permission to perform all the evil intents his totally perverse heart could render completely bewilders us. We are as the holy angels who cover their faces in God's presence. The active demonstration of God's love in permitting Satan's request so we could be the beneficiaries brings us to our knees and, as was true for Job, places our hands over our mouths. In the case of Job, God placed restrictions on Satan in that he could not murder Job; with Jesus there was no such limitation. The Godhead intervened and stopped Abraham from sacrificing his own son Isaac; there would be no intervention tonight with His own beloved Son Jesus. How could God permit such suffering to be inflicted, even on His own Son? If you can beggar an inkling of an answer—and you must answer this before you demand a response from God as to why you suffer when He can prevent it—then you have a small glimpse into how God's mind and heart works, as well as the unreachable depths of His love. Such divine wisdom and love are simply too high for us. Try as we may we cannot put ourselves in God's position. Our sin nature makes comprehension of holiness in thought or deed only observable when God displays it; we cannot intellectually or experientially bring ourselves to the point where we can attain or understand it. But God could, and God did, and He took the events of that one fateful night and changed eternity forever.

With this biblical foundation let us return to First Peter to see what and why Peter wrote to his suffering believers. We saw in First Peter 1:5 he informed the saints that they were "protected by the power of God through faith for a salvation ready to be revealed in the last time." But this is not his entire explanation. In the next verse Peter explained, "In this you greatly rejoice, even though now for a little while, if necessary, you have been distressed by various trials" [*peirasmos*]. We have a good idea of the source of the trials too. More specifically and with a more expanded disclosure, Peter further counseled his trembling flocks, "Do not be surprised at the fiery ordeal among you, which comes upon you for your testing [*peirasmos*] as though some strange thing were happening to you" (4:12). It makes more sense now, does it not? We are aligned with Him whom Satan hates, and we receive some of the same abuse He Himself received. It helps explain why "I was minding my own business and walking with God, when all these things happened to me!" If you were not walking with God and faithful to Him, you would have no reason to be the object of Satan's disdain.

Peter had more to teach us about fiery ordeals. First Peter 4:13 is a continuation of the "do not be surprised" verse of 4:12 and shows how God views this type of suffering: "but to the degree that you share the sufferings of Christ, keep on rejoicing, so that also at the revelation of His glory, you may rejoice with exultation." Each component of this verse is rich in imagery and information. The phrase "to the degree" is necessary, especially when we consider the totality of what Jesus suffered. Peter could not write, "Just as you suffer as Christ did"—it would not be accurate. No one has or ever could suffer what Christ did. God would never allow it, and even more to the point, we could never qualify. We know experientially only a most limited degree of His suffering, but even experiencing that lesser degree changes us forever. The word "share" is an old friend to us, being the verb form of *koinonia*, the noun Paul used for "fellowship" in Philippians 3:10: "that I may know Him . . . and the fellowship of His sufferings." When Peter wrote, "to the degree you share the sufferings of Christ," he wrote the same thing Paul did. It could be translated, "To the degree you have shared fellowship in the sufferings of Christ." God is amazingly consistent throughout His Word. Instead of concluding that we suffer alone, we see that God views our suffering with the same interest and concern He did Christ's. As before, "sufferings," are plural, as they are in describing "the sufferings first and the glories to follow" (1 Peter 1:11), the temptations of Jesus (Luke 22:28), and "He learned obedience from the things (plural) He suffered" (Heb. 5:8). Sufferings related to the *peirasmos* testings were plural to Him, and they will be with us too—but what holy and regal company we have in the midst of our sufferings.

While not the total answer, First Peter 4:19 summarizes for us what our present perspective should be: "Therefore, let those also who suffer according to the will of God entrust their souls to a faithful Creator in doing what is right." Peter had heard Jesus pray, "Thy will be done, on earth as it is in heaven." He had also witnessed and heard the agony of "Let this cup pass from Me! Nevertheless, not what I will, but what Thou will." Could he write otherwise regarding God's sovereignty in his own life that would soon end? Could he offer any other counsel to his suffering flocks? He—as they—was to suffer according to the will of God. This did not automatically mean to suffer unto death, as is evident with Job, whose suffering ended with his life regaining its fullness. But, it did mean to suffer according to God's will, whatever His specific will is for each individual life. In essence, it is the same dictum Peter received from Jesus when Peter asked what would be the future course for John. To paraphrase Jesus, "That is none of your business; only mine. You do not wonder about or look to him—you follow Me." Years later Peter would write the same. "Do not look to me, Peter, as the source of encouragement or example, look to Him, Jesus." The readers (and we) are to "entrust their souls to a faithful Creator," again having Jesus as our example and forerunner.

In the earlier passage of First Peter 2:21 we saw Jesus left a *hypogrammon* example for us to follow on in His steps, and we saw what a powerful passage that was. However, this verse offers us additional insight. In the same passage Peter wrote of Jesus, "Who committed no sin; nor was any deceit found in His mouth; and while being reviled, He did not revile in return, while suffering, He uttered no threats, but kept entrusting Himself to Him who judges righteously." Part of following in the steps of Jesus is to endure and trust God in our response to *peirasmos* trials that cause suffering. We must respond by faith, entrusting both our souls and the outcome to Him, just as Jesus did. We must do so without knowing the outcome beforehand, which is another way of saying we are to walk by faith. You will find that doing so, especially if the suffering is prolonged, is vastly harder than most people realize, but the only sure and safe course in the long run.

Stop figuring out why. Follow instead the Pathfinder and Forerunner of our sufferings.

So only months before his own martyrdom, Peter's counsel to his fellow-sufferers was, "Do not be surprised at the fiery ordeal that comes upon you for your testing." The victory is won, but the battles continue. We acknowledge this concept in theory, but it still surprises us when suffering surrounds us—but it really should not. The servant is not above his Master. We are sharers of His suffering, and will be sharers of His glory. Not only should we actively endure by trusting God, but also if we get our perspective in line with God's, the result of such suffering can be a matter of great joy for us. The joy goes beyond simply having the suffering end. Even beyond these other considerations is one underlying truth we need to explore: God uses *peirasmos* trials for the express purpose so He may bless us.

Chapter Eight

The Blessing

To various degrees most Christians desire to know God and have fellowship with Him. We want Jesus not only to be our Savior, but also our Leader, Protector, Provider, and Friend. We want Him to guide and direct our paths, to show us His divine will in our lives. God both commands and commends us for doing so. After all, what biblical option do we have? If we replaced any role of God with ourselves or someone else, it would be sinful. Condensed to its simplest level, we desire God's blessing. We want—and need—to be blessed by God.

Jacob realized this. In an unusual account in Genesis 32, Jacob wrestled with a Man, whom he later realized was actually God Himself. After wrestling with Him all night and having his hip joint dislocated, Jacob refused to let go of the Man until God blessed him. God granted his request by responding, "Your name shall no longer be Jacob, but Israel; for you have striven with God and with men and have prevailed" (Gen. 32:28). Jacob received God's blessing, marveling, "I have seen God face to face, yet my life has been preserved" (32:29-30).

This encounter intrigues us because of its sheer ludicrousness: God wrestled with Jacob. Why would God Almighty wrestle with anyone? Not only that, but also this account concerned one individual in ancient history. Can we learn anything from this event thousands of years later, particularly in reference to receiving God's blessing? Surprisingly we can make a few pertinent observations, and as usual, they are not what we would associate with blessings from God. For instance, in Jacob's case God did not merely hand His blessing to Jacob: Jacob had to exhibit great effort and endurance to receive it. Also, God had to bring Jacob to the point of becoming a vessel fit for blessing, and Jacob by no means enjoyed the process. Besides this, while God blessed after the battle had ended, Jacob came away changed for life. Scripture does not reveal if Jacob's hip joint ever healed. He very well may have walked the rest of his life with a limping reminder of his encounter with—and his blessing from—God.

Yet beyond these truths, the foundational question remains: Why would God wrestle with any mortal? Obviously, God could have destroyed Jacob without even appearing in person. If it were God's intent, He could have killed Jacob instantly by the sheer glory of His presence. But still, back to the question at hand, why would God wrestle with anyone, especially one whom He loves? Jacob was the grandson of Abraham, and heir to the covenant promises. His lineage would consist of the twelve tribes of Israel and eventually even the Christ. The entire Jewish nation would take its name from Jacob's new name Israel, a name specifically given to him by God after they wrestled. When you consider it, little about this encounter matches our understanding of God. His presence and blessing, yes, but wrestling, no. Wrestling is usually against one's adversary, not one's benefactor, and a prolonged, frustrating, and perhaps even painful wrestling at that. At the very least Jacob certainly experienced pain in the dislocation of the socket of his thigh. Casual reading of this episode may suggest it was God's purpose to inflict pain and frustration instead of blessing. It seems as though blessing had to be pried out of His hand, with God bestowing this only begrudgingly. We usually do not associate wrestling with receiving blessing from God. Yet blessing must have been God's intent, otherwise, He never would have appeared to Jacob in the first place.

Before moving on to related passages we can glean a few more applications concerning blessing in our own lives. We must, however, approach this cautiously. God dealt with Jacob in a unique situation. He is under no obligation to deal with us in the same manner any more than He is to make a covenant with us as He did with Abraham or place a star in heaven announcing our birth. We must be careful in assuming God has specific lessons for us to learn from Jacob's account that go beyond the bounds He intends. We can, however, learn from this example. We can see in this case—and very likely others—God forced someone aligned with Him to wrestle against Him. He may require the same of us. If such wrestling does occur, it does not necessitate a physical wrestling. In Ephesians 6:12, Paul wrote, "we wrestle not with flesh or blood," but against demonic forces, which obviously are not physical beings. Wrestling may be in the spiritual realm, primarily seen in one's prayer life and tenacious endurance in clinging to God despite all contrary circumstances. While not answering all related questions, it would explain why sometimes God seems to be an adversary against us instead of a sustainer. In a limited sense, and stated with the proper reverence, God may choose to take on an adversary's role for a particular time. By no means does God do this in the full scope available to Him, and not with the intent to destroy us. Purpose always lies at the heart of all God's activities. However, if wrestling with God does occur, it takes a vastly greater effort than when God undergirds and uplifts us. Even in the physical realm, an opponent who possesses superior strength greatly restricts your movement. Merely enduring the wrestling match, let alone winning, requires great exertion. Weariness because of the prolonged nature of the wrestling ensues. Physical wrestling in Jacob's case lasted all night. No time limits are given if one wrestles spiritually with God. Also, such a grueling undertaking demands a determined resolve. Thoughts about giving up, it not being worth it, and dull discouragement must have crossed Jacob's mind, as they will ours, if we wrestle an extended period with God. Lastly, God wore down Jacob and changed him so he could receive blessing. Jacob would never again be the same after this episode with God. We should expect similar effects, especially in receiving the deeper blessings of God. In its simplest terms, Jacob never would have become the blessed Israel if he had not striven with God and endured. It demonstrated to God—and especially to Jacob—how important God's blessing was to him.

We should not conclude that the account of Jacob in Genesis 32 contains all the information concerning blessings from God. This is only one of many examples where God required patient endurance necessary for Him to work His plan as well as bless the participants. Other examples include Abraham waiting years for God to give him the promised heir, Joseph languishing for years in an Egyptian prison, Moses' forty-year exile as a shepherd in Midian, Ruth gleaning the fields in her grief and misery, David being anointed the king of Israel and yet sent back to shepherd the sheep—and on and on the list goes. Rarely in Scripture, if at all, does one receive great blessings of God or is one used tremendously by Him without wrestling with God through pain, disappointment, despondency, loneliness, or suffering. Although quite painful during the process, all such prolonged testing occurs for the express purpose of God refining and blessing us.

Beyond such Old Testament examples, we have New Testament passages that teach the same biblical truths even more clearly. Scripture plainly states suffering can be used of God to accomplish great blessing in the lives of those He loves—which includes us—if responded to properly. Among other places, we find this in the lives and writings of Peter and James.

Peter knew firsthand what it was to be blessed of God, Jesus having pronounced him so on at least two occasions. The Greek word for "blessed" is *makarios*, which originally meant "happy." Over the years the word came to mean "religious happy," that is, one who enjoys particular divine favor. In one example Peter was among the twelve when the religious leaders of Israel publicly renounced Jesus. It was then Jesus began speaking to the multitudes in parables, partly to hide truth and partly to reveal it. In contrast to the religious leaders who would have no part of this presumed charlatan presenting himself as Israel's promised Messiah, Jesus told the twelve, "Blessed [*makarios*] are your eyes because they see; and your ears, because they hear" (Matt. 13:16). No doubt, the disciples were "religious happy." God blessed them by revealing the spiritual truths of His Gospel, longed for by the Old Testament prophets, but rejected by the current leaders of Israel. Weeks later Jesus addressed Peter with the same designation, but this time it was for him alone. Matthew 16:17 records one of Peter's warmest and yet most painful memories of his association with Jesus. After Peter declared Jesus was the Christ, the Son of the living God, Jesus continued, stating, "Blessed [*makarios*] are you, Simon Barjona, because flesh and blood did not reveal this to you, but My Father who is in heaven." Of course, the pain came with the rebuke by Jesus only moments later when Peter attempted to hinder Jesus from heading toward the cross. That was a lot for a Jewish fisherman to accept in one day—pronounced blessed because of the revelation given him by God the Father, and then rebuked by the Messiah when Peter spoke as a mouthpiece for Satan's work. So Peter knew of what being blessed of God consisted, and he would be very selective whenever stating someone else was in that category.

At face value then, how odd are the two instances Peter used in his epistles for one being blessed by God. When Peter wrote to his fellow-sufferers in First Peter 3:14, he informed them, "But even if you should suffer for the sake of righteousness, you are blessed" [*makarios*]. He does not say, "Suffer and you will eventually be blessed," but rather they were already in a state of blessedness. Later in 4:14 Peter repeated essentially the same concept, stating, "If you are reviled for the name of Christ, you are blessed" [*makarios*]. As with virtually everything else related to suffering, this surprises us. With Jacob we can partially understand blessing following wrestling with God, and with Job we can perceive of blessing following suffering or trials. We have a difficult time, however, deducing we are presently blessed in the midst of suffering. We may be able to see benefits coming out of any trial we endure, but consider it blessing? Keep rejoicing to the degree you share the sufferings of Christ? It is not our natural human response.

While we will come back to these and other related verses, such a concept of blessing linked with trials and suffering should not be all that foreign to us. In the first recorded public sermon by Jesus, the Sermon on the Mount, Jesus began with nine beatitudes, each beginning with *makarios*. We agree in principle to "Blessed are the gentle, for they shall inherit the earth," or "Blessed are the merciful, for they shall receive mercy." Yet, some beatitudes do not align with our understanding of blessing. For instance, "Blessed are those who have been persecuted for the sake of righteousness, for theirs is the kingdom of heaven." When, or if, persecution occurs, most of us do not consider ourselves blessed. Try this one: "Blessed are you when men cast insults at you, and persecute you, and say all kinds of evil against you falsely, on account of Me." Most of us would not conclude, "I can tell I'm blessed of God because of the persecution against me!" It simply does not fit our mentality. Nothing about it matches what we expect regarding God's blessings.

One reason this is so incompatible with our way of thinking is our definition of blessing often differs considerably from God's definition of blessing. While our perception of blessing may have a spiritual element to it, most of us view blessings from God largely in the earthly or physical realm: health, safety, possessions, etc. Again, these are valid to a degree, and we should look to God as our Provider and Giver. But God has a more elevated perception of blessing. God sees the total scope of future history, looking at eternal consequences, whereas we are mostly limited, both by choice and by design, to the temporal. For example, while we often define blessings mostly in pleasant physical circumstances ("God has really blessed my business"), God's blessings originate in the spiritual realm. Paul wrote believers are "blessed with every spiritual blessing in the heavenly places in Christ" (Eph. 1:3). He used a different word for "blessed," *eulogeo*, meaning "to bless or to endow." It is where we get our word eulogy. Paul might have used this word since his focus was on the Person of God and what He gives in blessing, rather than on us as recipients. In any event, the spiritual basis exists. I often asked my students, "Would you rather have a physical blessing from God or a spiritual one?" With the best intentions most students replied they desired a spiritual blessing. However, it is not as easy as one may think. What if you were losing use of your legs or eyes? Would you rather have a physical blessing or a spiritual one? What if you do not have the money to pay the rent or buy groceries or take your children to the doctor? Would you rather have a spiritual blessing or a physical one? Add what you will to the list, if we stripped down the externals of our souls, most of us would rather have a spiritual blessing with some sort of physical tag attached to it. Again, this is not necessarily bad, especially since we live in a world that requires physical provisions. But, an overemphasis on the material is at odds with how God views blessing. God sees the complete picture and can therefore see blessings He has ahead of us, as well as the route He must take us to bring us there, even when we see only darkness. Yet, this very process adds to our confusion because most of our sufferings involve the loss of something or someone precious to us. Since our perception of blessing often relates largely to physical matters, the temporary removal of such physical blessings intensifies our suffering. It causes us to consider ourselves anything but blessed of God. We can perceive God's blessing in the lives of others, but sometimes it is hard to see it in our own lives, especially in the midst of deep suffering. As always, we need to have our perception broadened by God's Word.

In the previous chapter we saw how *peirasmos* trials often originate from Satan, with the evil intent of having us fail and fall. Another word for testing, *dokimion*, shows an entirely different purpose. A *dokimion* testing reveals the value or quality of the thing tested; a testing to show something is genuine or worthy. While *peirasmos* is usually associated with Satan, *dokimion* is virtually always associated with God. While God will not lead one into sin, He will most definitely stretch one's faith through a *dokimion* testing. God's command to Abraham to sacrifice his son Isaac is a good example of God testing the faith He knew was present. God did not discover Abraham's faith; Abraham bore evidence of the faith already resident within him. Having two different words for trials or testing enables us to understand the nature of many trials and suffering. It demonstrates Satan is not always responsible for the trials that come upon us; God Himself may test our faith. Realizing the Bible uses two different words for trials reinforces that we may not be able to determine if our tests originate from God or Satan. Having the origin of some trials remain indeterminate may very well be God's design. Since we may never know the source, our emphasis should not be so much on determining the trial's origin, as it should be on responding to it properly. Despite its origin we must respond to the trial the same, in faithful obedience and submission to God. That must be our focus and drive.

Contrary to what we may think, the same trial can be at once both a *peirasmos* and a *dokimion* testing. Peter used both words in addressing the trials and suffering of his readers: "In this you greatly rejoice, even though now for a little while, if necessary, you have been distressed with various trials [*peirasmos*], that the proof [*dokimion*] of your faith, being more precious than gold which is perishable, even though tested by fire, may be found to result in praise and glory and honor at the revelation of Jesus Christ" (1 Peter 1:6-7). James 1:2-3 states virtually the identical truth: "Consider it all joy, my brethren, when you encounter various trials [*peirasmos*], knowing that the testing [*dokimion*] of your faith produces endurance." We have seen James 1:13 indicates one is not tested [*peirasmos*] by God into sin, so this is an example where God can use for His benefit— and for ours—trials brought upon Christians. Just this one simple distinction is helpful. God allows tests in our lives for us to pass, not looking for us to fail. For instance, we claim we have faith in God. God allows or brings tests on us in which we may give evidence of the genuineness of our faith. Such tests, however, move us far beyond our comfort zone. The "proof of your faith" will stretch you in ways you never have been, and in ways you never knew you could. We err, however, if we conclude that since God wants us to pass the test, the testing will be easy and the results guaranteed. Many have failed the *dokimion* testing God gave and suffered the consequences of their disobedience. God's testing of our faith looks for us to pass, but there is no assurance we will. Success comes only when one progresses with faith, courage, and obedience to God. Otherwise certain failure awaits.

Before dealing with other particulars of these verses, we need to meet the author of the Epistle of James. Since James wrote about suffering and the proper way we should respond, it would behoove us to understand a little about his background. For one thing, this James is not the brother of John, but instead the half-brother of Jesus (same mom, different dad). Since Mark 6:3 indicates townspeople regarded Jesus as "the son of Mary, and brother of James," and the same passage lists other brothers and sisters, James must have been the one born next after Jesus, that is, the next to the oldest son. Mark 3:21 states early in the earthly ministry of Jesus, His own relatives (with no doubt the exclusion of Mary and Joseph, if Joseph was still alive then), were embarrassed by Him to the point of action: "And when His own kinsmen heard of this [of the masses following Jesus], they went out to take custody of Him; for they were saying, 'He has lost His senses.'" James may very well have been with the group, in spirit at least, if not physically present. It would have been quite difficult to share a room, meals, bathroom facilities or work with someone whom many would eventually call the Christ, the Son of the Living God. "That was God in the flesh who slept beside me all those years?" Too deep for a simple man from Galilee to comprehend, and no doubt James—whose Old Testament equivalent of his name was Jacob—wrestled with God about this. From decades of living with Him, James knew Jesus was unique, but the Messiah, the promised One of Israel? It was a wrestling that lasted years. James would become one of the last converts of Jesus before His Ascension, most likely becoming a believer when Jesus made a special post-resurrection appearance to him (1 Cor. 15:7).

While it may thrill us to think about growing up alongside Jesus, in some ways it would have been extremely burdensome for James. No angels appeared to James explaining what had happened or who Jesus was. Of all the brothers in Israel, it was James' lot to end up with One who was perfect. No one ever had a son like Jesus, and no one ever had an older brother like Him either. Talk about how hard it was to live up to your older brother's standard! "Come clean your room, Jesus!"—"Already cleaned, Mom!" or, "Well, James, let's see what you made for your science project. Well, isn't that cute, Joseph! James made a little clay ducky. Now let's look at what Jesus made for His." Of course, Jewish boys of that day did not make science projects, but what a project Jesus could have made if He had so desired. It would be interesting to know whether Mary ever cast the painful barb at James, "Why can't you be more like your older brother?" She probably never said this—she knew why James could not.

Because of such strains as these, or maybe for other reasons, James did not initially receive Jesus for anything other than whom he knew Him to be: his older brother. Period. So Jesus did not choose James to be one of His Twelve; James was not ready or capable at that time in his life. If James followed Jesus against his will, James, too, might have even followed Judas' tragic course of disbelief. Whatever contact James had with Jesus during the Gospel accounts is left to speculation since his first mention as a believer occurs in the Book of Acts. Yet one curious aspect is evident from the silence of the Gospels: James was absent from Jesus' crucifixion. Mary was there, but not James. The dying Jesus commended care of His mother to John, yet James was the next son in line. Perhaps Jesus could only fully commit Mary to one who intimately knew who He was and what He was doing. Mary's grief would be such it would require more than the sustaining support of a physical son; it necessitated a brother in the faith. When we get to heaven, we will discover where James was when Jesus was being crucified. Was he unintentionally delayed from being in Jerusalem (yet it was Passover, the entire nation came to a standstill and gathered in Jerusalem)? Was he in supreme embarrassment because of the shame Jesus placed on their family, especially in the humiliating public death by crucifixion? Or maybe something else happened. Perhaps James did attend the crucifixion but kept his presence unknown to others, especially Mary. Did he blend in with the masses, partly hidden by the darkness that surrounded the earth during the crucifixion? And if by chance James did sneak up to the crucifixion, did he come close enough to make eye contact with Jesus? Would it have the same effect on him as the look of Jesus on Peter? Would James understand even partially what his older Brother—and ultimately His God—was doing? Pure speculation. We have no way of knowing, but it is intriguing.

What we do know is James changed forever when he encountered the resurrected Jesus. Scripture does not reveal the exact time frame, but if James had not believed in Jesus before the resurrection, James was the only unbeliever to whom Jesus appeared after He rose from the grave. Whatever happened, we know this: James became not only a faithful follower of Jesus; he became a useful instrument as well. James became the leader of the home church of Jerusalem, an extremely strategic church, since it was the hub from which the Gospel spread. While Jesus commissioned the apostles to go out unto the utter most part of the earth, the home church required a solid leader to shepherd the flock. They chose James, not because Jesus was his half-brother, but because James gave overwhelming evidence that Jesus was his Lord.

Not only did James pastor the Jerusalem church, but also chronologically, James wrote the first New Testament book—and James came out swinging. The general theme throughout his epistle is, "You call yourself a Christian? Here are some tests by which you can measure the faith you claim you have"—and they are difficult tests indeed. To James, talking a good game about being a believer meant nothing. A believer's faith should be alive and evident to all. A living faith can be evaluated in response to the trials and testing one encounters, evidence of good works in one's life, control of one's tongue, prayer, keeping oneself undefiled by the world, and many other evidences. Most people do not feel wonderful about themselves after reading his epistle; it was not James' intention that they would. James did not want people happy; he wanted them holy. James would not be a modern day sympathetic counselor. Someone who approached James and conceded, "James, James, I don't know where I will get the money I need!" might have received the response, "You do not have because you do not ask. You ask and you do not receive, because you ask with wrong motives, so that you may spend it on your pleasures" (James 4:2-3). If you approached James and complained of your suffering, he would have a one-word response: pray! (5:13). No toots and whistles or psychological profiles. James smacks us directly and repeatedly with the point he makes. Sometimes we need a James in our lives to remove our veneer and force us to examine the deep recesses of our own hearts.

Yet, James also had a tender side to him. He understood not only the origin and distinctions of trials, especially trials of suffering, but also the process God intends for the believer to follow. While much of what he writes is in harmony with Peter, it differs at its heart. Whereas Peter repeatedly pointed to the suffering of Jesus and how believers should follow His example, James never does. Perhaps James reasoned since he had not witnessed firsthand the sufferings of Jesus, he did not deem himself worthy to use Jesus as the example he himself had once disavowed. All this was no doubt part of God's grand design. Peter did witness the sufferings of Christ (1 Peter 5:1) and continually directed the readers to Him. James did not, and he continually pointed to the believer's own responsibility to endure by faith. Both approaches are needed to give balance. One who meets suffering and glibly responds, "God will give me strength," may be in for a jolt at the depth and intensity of the suffering. On the other hand, one who attempts to suffer only in the strength of the flesh will also quickly meet with failure and discouragement; a higher Person, strength and grace must be operative. God knew we needed both teachings to endure properly, and He inspired both writers accordingly.

So while certainly not denying God's presence or resources in the midst of one's trials, James emphasized the role of the believer. To James, the believer should respond to trials with faithful endurance. In James 1:12 he wrote, "Blessed is a man who perseveres under trial." The Greek word for "persevere" is quite picturesque, being derived from the combination *hypo*, meaning "under," and the verb *meneo*, meaning, "to abide." The combined form equates endurance with "abiding under." The noun form is *hypomenes*, repeatedly translated in Scripture as "endurance" or "steadfast endurance." It was one of Paul's favorite words, and he used it in reference to multiple aspects of the Christian walk where faithful endurance was needed. The word conveys action, not passivity. "Abiding under" is not a defeatist attitude of hopeless acquiescence, but rather an active abiding under the trial with faith in God as one's base. Consequently James' thought is, "Blessed is the man who *hypomenes* endures under trial." For him, such endurance was the foremost responsibility of believers in the midst of their trials. Before examining deeper considerations of suffering, James will always bring us back to this initial question: "Are you currently abiding under whatever trial God has allowed into your life?" If you are not, you need to be. You cannot advance any farther until you do.

We can see how *hypomenes* endurance is necessary when one suffers, but we should not conclude it occurs automatically. Most of us do not seek "to abide under" suffering when it comes our way. Instead, we seek a way out, which is the normal human response. It does not seem wrong or illogical to attempt to alleviate any suffering you are able. However, some sufferings come upon you that you can never remove from your life, such as the death of a loved one or being stricken with a lifelong disability. Still merely being in a trial is not the same as actually abiding under it. One can be in the midst of suffering, have no way out of it, and yet not "abide under" it. One can hold resentment toward God for what He has done, or at least in their estimation of what He has done. While begrudging believers cannot change their circumstances, neither do they abide under what God has allowed to come their way. A stubborn resistance of the heart and will embraces them. *Hypomenes* endurance is not for cowards. It involves an active submission of the will and a trusting heart that reach beyond any present difficulties—but it is a prerequisite for God to bestow deeper blessings. In fact, James begins his epistle with this teaching. "Consider it all joy, my brethren, when you encounter various trials [*peirasmos*], knowing the testing [*dokimion*] of your faith produces endurance [*hypomenes*]" (James 1:2-3). God produces endurance—we do not. God specifically and precisely works in our lives to produce the *hypomenes* endurance we would not be able to manufacture by our own efforts. He does this as we properly respond to our trials, much in the same way one grows stronger physically by lifting objects heavier than during the normal routine of life. We purposefully do it with physical exercise; God purposefully directs our spiritual exercise. Not only that, but James 1:4 indicates without this trait, one is not as fully developed as God intends: "And let *hypomenes* endurance have its perfect result, that you may be perfect and complete, lacking in nothing." This verse clearly shows God has a distinct goal and purpose He seeks to accomplish through the testing of our faith. Our responsibility is to submit and endure, often the two most difficult Christian virtues to achieve. How interesting that Job, chronologically the first Old Testament book, and James, the first of the New Testament, both address believers enduring trials and suffering. Maybe God still has much to teach our consumer-conscious modern Christianity. We have a great deal to learn from James, and from the Good Shepherd, about trials and sufferings that we encounter.

We should note at this point that the previous truths are primarily for self-examination instead of evaluating how others respond to their trials. Go easy when invading the domain of someone else's suffering. "Abiding under" what God has allowed to take place may be the most difficult effort one has ever attempted, and it may be something God enables the believer to be able to do in time. It may take a while, but God is a most patient teacher. Intercessory prayer often helps far more than advice.

James realized *hypomenes* endurance goes beyond what we would and could bring about by our own efforts. We also would curtail the exercise, if we could, long before God does. Our inclination is usually to give up—give up in hope anyway, if not actually in deed—long before God stops the process. As a means of encouragement, James reminded his readers of the beneficial aspects of enduring suffering as seen in the lives of the Old Testament prophets. In James 5:10 he wrote, "As an example, brethren, of suffering and patience, take the prophets who spoke in the name of the Lord." Here is a concept we understand but do not like to apply to ourselves. Faithful and useful servants of God in the Old Testament had to endure suffering patiently. In fact, often the higher the status of the prophet in the Old Testament, the more intense his suffering. Most endured tremendous hardships. It is easier to expect this in someone else's life than it is our own. Also, James used two articles in front of suffering and patience. In other words "As an example, brethren, of the suffering and the patience"—both specific entities, not ethereal concepts. James does not refer to merely suffering and patience in general, but the suffering and the patience specifically brought about for those who walk deeply with God. God greatly used such faithful servants; He still can with us as well. Much of what we have in the Bible is due to the prophets' steadfast endurance. They are examples of not only how God can use someone, but also the faithful endurance required for God to work as He wills. God has not altered this fundamental requirement for deeper blessing, despite the "me-centered Christianity" that has invaded much of the world.

James 5:11 contains other factors we need to consider: "Behold, we count those blessed who [hypomenes] endured." A few points within this verse help us in our understanding of suffering. As always, the little word "behold," should not be readily skipped over. It calls attention to the importance of what is about to be stated. By appropriating this verse we can see more clearly a purpose behind our suffering, as well as the need for endurance. We may not have the total picture or understand why us, but we do understand God has a distinct purpose in our suffering. God is in the process of developing certain spiritual qualities within us that would not be there otherwise, such as steadfast endurance. But, we can also look forward to God blessing us once we have achieved the approval [dokimion]. As with Jacob we are brought to the point where God can bestow blessings on us, some physical, some spiritual, but all originating from His generous and gracious hand. Such truth should be a source of comfort and hope in the midst of our suffering, but again, this does not happen without a concentrated effort to submit to God. Praying to God for help or relief should be done, especially in view of His compassion and mercy, something we long for when suffering comes our way. Yet, God's will may indeed be that we abide under some or all of the particular trials before us. God is not uncaring or incapable of intervening in our behalf. He is simply waiting for the proper time once the test is over, *hypomenes* endurance produced, and our faith approved. Instead of abandonment in the midst of our trials, God continually transforms us closer and closer to the image of His Son, fitting us for a deeper walk and greater blessing.

Another aspect of this verse is helpful to me personally. The King James Version translates James 5:11 as, "You have heard of the patience of Job." Actually, the word for "patience" is again *hypomenes*, being correctly translated, "You have heard of the endurance of Job." Several times throughout the book, Job gave evidence that he was not very patient, but then again, neither would we be if we endured his trials. Job experienced both peaks and valleys, as is normal in intense suffering. Job stated he would trust God if He would slay him, and yet if God were a man Job would accost Him to his face. He knew his Redeemer lives, but felt the agonizing absence of His presence. Job looked for God, but he could not find Him. Pinnacles and pits, light and darkness, hope and gloom. It is encouraging to me because we will most likely experience the same range of response, especially if our suffering lasts a lifetime. Remember though, Job never denied or abandoned God. Though frustrated to his limit, Job clung to God as tightly as Jacob did—and we must also. At times you will respond joyously, at times the dull ache of darkness and misery will engulf you. At times you will see God's hand actively at work, at others you will pine for His delightful presence you enjoyed in days gone by. It is an arduous journey, and it can be quite lonely and discouraging, even when surrounded by loved ones. Often the pain is compounded when well-meaning friends tell us, "Well, just be patient as Job was." It hurts because patience may not be at the forefront of our character qualities, but it would not be for many of those offering counsel either. Prolonged suffering beats you down. How you responded to suffering earlier may not be the same as you do later, as evident by comparing Job's initial response to suffering ("Shall we indeed accept good from God and not accept adversity?" Job 2:10) with his multiple complaints throughout the remainder of the book. This does not mean we should shake our fist in God's face in defiance. But, it does mean God understands the development of *hypomenes* endurance is a painful process, and pain often produces whimpering and complaining. We do not surprise God in our spiritual valleys. He meets us there—more to the point—He brought us there. He understands if others who offer such counsel were so inflicted, they would have their valleys too.

While suffering maintains many mysteries still not revealed to us, we do have enough understanding to put into a lifetime of practice. Our responsibility is to abide under by faith the particular trials before us, even when we feel like giving up. If wrestling with God is our lot, we must wrestle and hang on tenaciously until that test ends. Instead of plotting ways out of suffering or attempting to figure out why us, we are to *hypomenes* endure by faith. We should exhibit the faith of the Old Testament prophets, but remember that it will cost us if we do. Suffering changes us; it always does, even as it did Jacob. It does not mean the road is easy—but it does mean the road is passable. If we allow God free reign and respond as He intends, suffering brings about transformational changes from the inside out. Along with the inward changes produced, we will see in the next chapter God's Word contains a special promise uniquely reserved for those who endure with *hypomenes* during their trials of suffering. In fact, we have His word on it.

Chapter Nine

The Agreement

Hurricane Fran ransacked North Carolina on September 6, 1996. My family lives in Wake Forest, just north of Raleigh. The last hurricane through this part of the state occurred over forty years before. State officials did not expect Fran to hit our section of the state, so we received relatively little warning. The storm arrived a little after midnight; officials closed public schools only two hours earlier. My arthritic joints quite accurately predicted the hurricane would hit us as I hobbled around the house all day. Earlier in the day my wife and two children hurried home at my insistence. We were in for a long night.

My daughter was a few days away from being eight years old, and my son six the night the hurricane arrived. They were pretty frightened. I do not know whether frightened best-described Betsy and me, but we were quite concerned. As soon as the storm hit we lost our electricity and the accompanying lights we so depend on every day, yet rarely acknowledge until they fail to work. We huddled the kids down in sleeping bags beside us on the first floor. We prayed together as the storm intensified. We spoke Bible verses to each other reminding each other of God's presence and protection.

I do not know whether it is better to go through a hurricane in the daytime or at night. If we could see much during the day, it would most likely alarm us. Lying awake at night during a hurricane most definitely brought great anxiety as sounds I never heard before sparked my imagination. In the blackest of black I heard the sounds of trees one foot in diameter snapped in half like toothpicks. Loud crashes of unknown origin occurred with much frequency. Tremendous thumps would startle us as broken limbs or other objects smashed into our house. The sound of the wind surrounded us. For some reason, I assumed the wind of a hurricane remained at a constant rate. To my surprise, the gusts would ebb and flow. They never receded much, but at times gusts would blow considerably harder than other times. One of the most memorable aspects was the sound our front door made. During such gusts, the door audibly "hummed." The stress against it caused by the wind made the chilling sound children make when they attempt to sound like a ghost. I expected the wind to break the door open and rip it from its hinges at any moment. For approximately four hours, Betsy and I lay by our kids as we listened to the devastation we knew was occurring but could not see.

Finally, an eerie silence awakened us. We had grown so accustomed to the roar of the wind, when it finally ceased, the quiet startled us. At the first peaks of sunlight, I went outside to view the damage left behind. I think most people responded as I did, thankful they received no injuries but dumbfounded with amazement at the extensiveness of the damage. Three of my neighbors had large trees across their houses. We lost over twenty trees, most of them quite large, but none hit our house. Entire neighborhoods looked similar to pictures of bomb scenes during a war. Uprooted and broken trees covered miles of streets and highways. One road we drove by disappeared from view as massive fallen oaks covered it, leaving debris over twenty feet high. The storm removed most items we take for granted. For many, no lights, no water, no phone would be their lot for weeks.

After the initial day or two of dazed acceptance, the reality of what the clean up and restoration would require sank in. Frustration and impatience became increasingly evident as people's patience waned. The late summer heat only added to the discomfort. Some things returned to normal relatively soon. Others would require months, or even years cleaning up as hundreds of thousands of trees had blown over. For a few people the storm changed their lives forever, removing something or someone from them that they never could replace.

Some people's lives are quite similar to being either in the midst of a hurricane or in the distressing and discouraging place of evaluating their damage immediately after the storm. Some are either just beginning or else in the midst of their suffering. Their storm still rages. They can hear the sounds and the crashes. They wonder if their spiritual front door will blow in and how long the storm will last. They conjecture how much damage will occur, and if they will survive. In the midst of the storm, however, is not the time to evaluate the damage. During the storm is the time to hold on to God, reminding themselves and others of His presence. For others, the event that caused the suffering or loss has already blown by. The dull heartache of evaluating their mammoth losses shows their worse fears are now a reality. Their loss is so great that they have no capacity to begin sorting out in their minds how to rebuild. In simplest terms, they cannot; it is too great a devastation for them to rebuild by themselves. For some, great personal loss and suffering have occurred which will alter their lives forever.

First Peter contains exhortations of hope if the storm of suffering has ravaged your life. The storm of which Peter speaks has a spiritual origin, but its devastation is just as noticeable physically as is that of a hurricane's. In fact, in First Peter 5:10, Peter chose words specifically describing rebuilding and repair as he presented a promise from God of what you can expect.

Many lawyers consider the closing remarks the most important aspect of a trial. They want the last words the jury hears to resonate in their thinking. Peter does as well. He did not write about a legal trial but rather various trials that come upon believers, fiery ordeals that surprise many, the degree they share the sufferings of Christ. Peter was not arguing for the release of a client. Instead, he based his case on the sufferings first and the glories to follow, encouraging the faithful to follow Jesus' example of obedient submission to the will of God. In First Peter 5:12 he charged the weary with his closing remark, "I have written to you briefly, exhorting and testifying that this is the true grace of God. Stand firm in it!" Standing firm requires abiding under what God allows in one's life, as well as maintaining the proper attitude.

In a sense, all First Peter is a closing argument to exhort the believers to stand firm in the faith. Peter built his case on existing truths for believers. Among other items, Peter reminded the readers that despite present circumstances, God currently protected them (1:5). Instead of considering trials and suffering as abandonment by God, Peter instructed them that such trials would result in praise and honor once their faith had been proven (1:6-7). The salvation believers possess is of such a magnitude, the angels of heaven have an intense desire to examine it (1:12). Salvation is what interests angels—not gold, fame, beauty, or anything else the world offers. No angel ever experientially received forgiveness or the transformation from defiled to cleansed, evil to holy. Since salvation is what intrigues them, angels most likely converse about its glories. We should too. Stand firm.

Interwoven throughout Peter's argument are the person and work of Jesus Christ. Peter had witnessed firsthand the sufferings of Christ (5:1) and could help explain Jesus to readers who never had yet seen Him (1:8), and that includes us. Peter repeatedly and consistently brought the readers' focus away from their problems to Jesus. The Good Shepherd knows and cares for His flock as no one else could, Himself being both Shepherd and Lamb. Suffering brings intense pain—it did for Him, too. The world is not fair—nor was it for Him. God allows Satan to buffet and harm us—He knows. Jesus knows by firsthand experience, and as omniscient God, He knows of their fiery ordeals. We cry out to God—Jesus did before we did. And on it goes. Jesus was the unblemished Lamb who submitted to God the Father. Trust and obedience were the basis for Jesus' relationship with God; we must walk in His footprints and follow His example. He struggled with sin—ours, not His own. Jesus is the Rock and guardian of our souls who died [*hyper*] in place of us. He is the Suffering Servant who watches over God's suffering servants. Look to Him. He loves and cares. Stand firm.

In a statement of encapsulation, Peter gave a fourfold promise of God to those who suffer. You must be quite confident of your call to tell someone, particularly someone in the midst of suffering, that God offers this promise. Multiplied heartaches await those whose hope for rescue is false. Peter had no such fear. He boldly set forth God's promise: "And after you have suffered for a little while, the God of all grace, who called you to His eternal glory in Christ, will Himself perfect, confirm, strengthen and establish you" (5:10). What a promise! At some specific, designated time in the future ("after you have suffered for a while") God will intervene. For those whose constant companion is suffering, First Peter 5:10 should become a friend. God wanted the first century suffering believers to know His promise. He still does today for His own. Stand firm.

Since this verse contains such a specific promise of great works of God, the human response usually speaks. "Well, that's great, but what is keeping Him so long? I believe (I think) He will intervene and rescue. But, how long must I suffer? When will God act on my behalf?" Good questions. You can count on God having better answers.

First Peter 5:10 was the verse in which I began my own studying on suffering. It has taken us eight chapters to get here. One of the items that first attracted me to this verse was Peter's word choice. He used four Greek words that describe rebuilding after devastation. Survivors of hurricanes and earthquakes will be quite familiar with the concept each word portrays and how each concept would be necessary. For those suffering intensely, hopes of God's restoration and strengthening are anointing oil on one's head. We will deal with each item of His promise shortly. However, as you probably realize by now, this verse contains more than we see at face value, and we must be good students of God's Word to mine the gold embedded within it. Initially we need to consider two related items. First, the verse begins with the word "and." "And" is a marker, pointing us backward to make sure we take all the information of the previous verses. Peter—and the Holy Spirit—did not intend for us to take this verse away from its context. The preceding verses contain information vital to our understanding and appropriating this promise, so we must begin there, not in First Peter 5:10. The second point relates to this: First Peter 5:10 speaks of God's role, His responsibility—responsibility that is, based on His promise. We never force God to do anything. He will, however, always follow through on doing what He said. Scripture cannot be broken. Once God has spoken He will always abide by His Word. However, First Peter 5:6-9 delineates the believer's role and responsibility. They give the requirements for the believer before addressing God's promises. We are prone to claim the promises of a verse like First Peter 5:10, and then wonder why God does not respond as we expect. We examine Him, but are less inclined to scrutinize our own lives, to strengthen our own weakness and adjust where needed, to continue in faith. Simply put, God's promises of rebuilding in 5:10 occur once the believer lives out the elements of 5:6-9. Our examination begins with ourselves—not with God—but remember, it leads to a promise. The sooner we get started, the sooner He intervenes.

In the verse before our section, First Peter 5:5, Peter instructed the young men of the churches to subject themselves to their elders. Everyone else was "to clothe themselves with humility toward each other." Peter reinforced his injunction by quoting Proverbs 3:34, "God is opposed to the proud, but gives grace to the humble." Jesus probably had Peter recite this verse a few hundred times a day. At one point in his life Peter was quite proud, as most of us are. Having grown in grace Peter now wrapped himself in the humility of knowing any hope and strength he possessed came only from the Lord. Humility is not an "Awe, shucks," self-abasement. True biblical humility consists of understanding who you are—and Whose you are—which when fully done, leads to reliance on His strength and grace. True humility does not say, "I can't do anything," but rather "I can do whatever God calls me to do through His power and leading—not my own." It took Peter years to learn this, but it is vital in walking with the Lord. Peter began his closing instruction on the believers' self-examination in 5:6 with the same principle, instructing believers to humble themselves under God. Our first requirement on our way to the promises of God in First Peter 5:10 is to humble ourselves, to abide under, to submit to God in trust. Such action is a statement of faith, especially in cases where you do not sense the presence of God. The humbling called for is not a broken-hearted giving up. Instead, it has God as its foundation and hope. We humble ourselves when we quit trying to explain our suffering and its origin, and instead stand firmly in faith, trusting God even when it makes no sense to us to do so. We humble ourselves when we walk by faith, not by sight, which means we will have to walk in the darkness. Walking by faith necessitates the need for direction; you must have a greater Light. When you humble yourself, you abandon all other sources for hope except for God.

Peter instructed the believers to humble themselves "under the mighty hand of God" (5:6). This designation of God has Old Testament roots and speaks of God's great delivering power. We need reminding of this when we suffer. Most know God could immediately intervene, just as Job knew. The strength of God was never the issue. Others, however, are not as spiritually strong. Their assessment of their situation is no one—including God—could untangle or repair their shattered lives. Peter again placed the emphasis on God. For some, trusting that God does, indeed, possess a "mighty hand" and that His strength is infinite may be a progression through which He leads them. Yet it is vital to arrive at this foundational point. Why humble yourself before a God who is no stronger than you or your spiritual enemy? He is, though, and He waits to show you. Humble yourself under His mighty hand. Stand firm.

Peter progressed from the humbling of oneself to the hope of exaltation. No doubt exists about Who will do the exalting. What a strange concept.

God is the One who deserves exalting, simply due to who He is or because of His mighty works. Yet He chooses to exalt those who humble themselves before Him. Actually, there is more to this verse. Many have the wrong concept of the transition from humbling to exaltation. Sometimes we sing in Christian gatherings, "Humble thyself in the sight of the Lord, and He will lift you up higher and higher." James 4:10 contains virtually the same wording and uses "and" to connect the two phrases. However, the Greek that Peter employed presents a subtle but distinct nuance. It is not "humble yourself and He will lift you up." The Greek word employed is translated "in order that" or "so that." Humble yourselves *in order that* He may exalt you. The verse does not call for a self-humbling and God will exalt, such as two weights balanced on a scale. Humbling oneself is necessary before God exalts. After all, why exalt someone who does not need it? It is not "do this and He will do this." Rather it is, "Do this—humble yourself—so that He can do this—exalt you."

While God is the One who exalts, often we intervene in an attempt to exalt ourselves, sometimes on a continual basis. It is human nature to do so. Peter called for something far beyond the world's normal procedures. He had learned the futility of self-exaltation the hard way. He heard Jesus rebuke the religious leaders of Israel in Matthew 23:12: "And whoever exalts himself shall be humbled; and whoever humbles himself shall be exalted." Peter, having both exalted himself and having likewise been humbled, believed these words. Decades later he used the same verb for "humble" in his instruction as Jesus had. Jesus spoke a statement of truth; Peter issued an injunction, a necessary prerequisite before God's exalting. While Jesus spoke against the arrogant religious leaders of His day, the same principle applies to everyone, believer and nonbeliever alike. Jesus spoke using indefinite pronouns: "And whoever exalts himself shall be humbled; and whoever humbles himself shall be exalted." Self-exaltation rarely, if at all works, and if it does, it is only temporary. Reverse logic applies also. If I exalt myself, God does not need to; if I do not, I must depend on someone else. God graciously chooses to intervene. One of the basal prerequisites for God to exalt you is that you humble yourself before Him. Such logic smacks against much of today's philosophy—secular, as well as some Christian—but it is biblically mandated all the same.

We understand what humbling ourselves requires, or at least we think we do. However, like children on a long trip, we, too, want to know how long will it take. How long do I humble myself before God exalts? God's answer parallels answers we give our children: until "the proper time," or colloquially translated, "when it is time" or "when it is ready." The Greek word means "in the due or appointed time." God will act to exalt us when in His infinite wisdom, it is conducive to His glory and our real welfare. A sign of true biblical humility is to wait patiently for God to respond, trusting that He knows when the time will be right. Part of the test comes with thinking the time of our testing is complete, when it is not, and then still looking in faith for God to act. He does not disclose when the proper time will be. It most likely varies for each individual, depending on the unique set of accompanying circumstances. We think in terms of hours and days; God's time is often years or decades. We must remember a large part of the timetable depends on how we respond. We may slow God's work by not humbling ourselves. Also, this is the section of Scripture that deals with the examination of ourselves—not an examination of Him. We need to make sure we are doing what God calls us to do and continue doing it until further notice.

"Casting all your anxiety," (5:7), is a pertinent term from a fisherman who understood a great deal about casting. This same word for casting was used for the garments cast upon the colt for the Triumphal Entry of Jesus (Luke 19:35). It is a participle in the Greek, which means it closely relates to the verb "humble yourselves" (1 Peter 5:6). In other words, one way "how do I know whether I am humbling myself?" can be answered is by seeing whether you have cast all your anxiety on the Lord. This verse strongly shows that humbling is not passively giving up or a self-resignation to defeat or disaster. Casting one's anxiety is an active statement of faith. Interestingly, Peter used the singular "all" in the Greek. It is though all your anxieties are to be bundled into one cluster and cast upon the Lord.

Also, surprisingly Peter did not use the present tense in Greek. This is important in understanding what the verse teaches. A present tense would indicate continuous action, which would make sense. When anxiety comes, you automatically pass it onto the Lord—continuous action. The tense Peter chose, however, indicates that the entire burden is to be cast on God in somewhat of an all-encompassing manner. This then points to a determined attitude, a once and for all settled conviction, which will show in how you deal with each episode of anxiety that comes your way. What the Bible calls for is difficult; it requires us to cast all anxiety on the Lord.

To hold some back is contrary to biblical humility. It means we are in reality plotting a way to rid ourselves of our source of suffering, if we can, instead of taking God at His Word that He will deal with it. Again, obedience is impossible without faith. Peter's rationale for such casting was "because He (God) cares for you." Sometimes accepting the fact God cares for you is particularly difficult to do. At times all outer circumstances of suffering seem to indicate that God does not do anything, especially actively care for us—but He does. True humility believes and accepts by faith that God lovingly and consistently works, even when we cannot see or feel any evidence that He does. Stand firm.

Attempts at reaching biblical humility will most assuredly be put to the test. After all, if these are the prerequisites for God's intervention, it makes sense Satan will do all he can to keep you from humbly submitting to God and casting your anxiety on Him. He may insinuate you deserve better; life—or God—is not fair. You followed God and look where it got you. Satan, the supreme slanderer and liar, will whisper lies that God has failed, He is not present, there is no hope for you—you are alone. Peter wanted his readers to be ready. The pending attack is just as certain for them as it was for Peter on the night of Christ's betrayal. If you humble yourself under God, you can count on the heat being turned up a few notches by the enemy.

Peter used two commands in 5:8 for proper spiritual preparation against the pending satanic attacks, namely, "be sober," and "be on the alert." The verbs give a sense of urgency that requires immediate attention. In each case, it is a call to warfare readiness. One should not assume past times of being sober or alert will suffice. Both verbs indicate a determined, settled mindset is in view. Once established, however, the nature of the attack necessitates continual vigilance. Peter placed both words at the beginning of the sentence for emphasis. "Sober," of course, in this context does not relate to alcohol, although alcohol could most certainly be a means of not being spiritually sober. This sobriety has to do with establishing a mindset of mental or spiritual alertness. Earlier in the epistle Peter wrote, "Therefore, gird your minds for action, keep sober in spirit, fix your hope completely on the grace to be brought to you at the revelation of Jesus Christ" (1:13). Again in 4:7 he exhorted, "The end of all things is at hand; therefore, be of sound judgment and sober spirit for the purpose of prayer." Three times Peter used "sober" in the sense of a proper mental awareness and perspective necessary for Christian faith in action. The final example calls for awareness of the spiritual enemy and battle at hand, especially in the midst of suffering.

"Watchful," *gregoreo* in the Greek, which is where we get our name "Gregory," is almost synonymous with "be sober." While translated "watchful," metaphorically it could be translated, "Wake up! Watch out! Pay attention!" This word would have been a bitter reminder for Peter, but one nonetheless needed by his readers. Matthew 26:37 states Jesus took Peter, James, and John with Him to the Gethsemane battleground. Jesus instructed the three, "My soul is deeply grieved, to the point of death; remain here and keep watch [*gregoreo*] with Me" (Matt. 26:38). In Matthew 26:40, at the end of the first round of battle prayer, Jesus returned and found the three sleeping. Interestingly, He addressed only Peter: "And He came to the disciples and found them sleeping, and said to Peter, "So, you men could not keep watch [*gregoreo*] with Me for one hour?" He further instructed them, "Keep watching [*gregoreo*] and praying that you may not enter into [*peirosmos*] temptation; the spirit is willing, but the flesh is weak." The disciple who had boasted he would stand with Jesus and never desert Him could not watchfully pray in Jesus' darkest hour—when, humanly speaking, Jesus needed him most. Peter expected to undertake heroic efforts to rescue Jesus. He refused, however, to believe the call of Jesus to watch prayerfully. Of course, lack of watchfulness only hastened Peter's failure. Throughout Scripture, though, Peter continually demonstrated one noble character trait: Peter was spiritually strong enough to learn from his past failures and then use them to warn others. The call for spiritual alertness he issued in writing First Peter 5:8 paralleled one of Peter's greatest failure. One needs a special grace to use one's most humiliating embarrassment as an example for others, yet Peter did. He loved his flock enough to warn them, much in the same way Jesus had admonished him.

As was true for his personal testing on that night, Peter linked the needed sobriety and watchfulness against the person and attacks of Satan. He does not define how satanic attacks occur. This is wise because Satan's schemes are too varied to describe. Peter instead placed emphasis on the believers' responsibility to resist. The means to accomplish this is the believer's faith, not personal faith as much as the content and truth of the Christian faith. First Peter 5:9, however, does reveal some of Satan's methodology. Since faith is the means to victory, and faith concerns that which is not seen, Satan counters by instilling doubts into the truthfulness of God and His Word. This works exceptionally well when one bases spiritual truth on one's observations only. Satan's methodology worked with Adam and Eve—it will also work with us, unless we are sober and watchful. Peter also gives us a glimpse into how serious Satan is. In 5:9 Peter wrote, "But resist him, firm in your faith, knowing that the same experiences of suffering are being accomplished by your brethren who are in the world." The same holds true today; nothing has changed. Throughout the entire world, those who walk with Jesus become targets of Satan's wrath. In our suffering, however, we often erroneously conclude we suffer alone. One day in heaven we will get to compare notes on suffering with believers throughout the ages. We will see different particulars and means, but we will see common fingerprints on much of our suffering.

We have now completed our spiritual checklist, our spiritual self-examination. If we maintain the divine commands of First Peter 5:1-9 daily, not sporadically, we do what God calls us to do. A brief review suffices. We humble ourselves. We cast our anxiety on Him; we recognize He cares for us. Satan's accusation against Job was that Job served God only for what God would give him. Whenever we cast our anxiety on God—rather than saying God does not care, or God is wrong for allowing us to have anxiety in the first place—we prove Satan wrong. But be ready for battle—Satan never loses graciously, nor is he inclined to give up easily. Consequently, the battle mandates a sober and watchful spirit. Even then we must resist his attacks that most certainly will come: attacks of despair, doubt, questioning God's motives—and on they go. Instead of deeming ourselves abandoned by God, God's Word instructs us to recognize the "same experiences of suffering are being accomplished by your brethren who are in the world" (5:9). Since suffering is often lengthy, it requires periodic, or even daily, examination, especially in suffering's darkest days.

Now comes God's part. Remember, First Peter 5:6 teaches God will intervene "at the proper time." God decides when that will be, not us. Put differently, God's actions, as defined in 5:10, will occur after the *dokimion* testing of our faith is over, and all the elements of 5:6-9 are an active part of our lives. Peter began 5:10 with the Greek word *de*, usually translated "but," instead of "and." "But" would be an appropriate translation here as well. Having spoken of the multiple requirements of the believers, he then contrasted these with what God will do. In fact, Peter emphasized God's role in this verse by the double naming of "God" and "Himself." Almost as rare as the use of Abba for God is the construction "God Himself." Only nine times in the entire New Testament does the term describe God. It depicts intimacy and closeness, a tenderness on God's part. God Himself, who knows and cares, will actively intervene in the midst of your suffering. Your renewal will not be due to your own efforts, a change of fortune, or simply "good luck." God Himself will actively intervene. It will be abundantly clear God Himself will work in such a way no doubt will exist that He is the source. What an unspeakable promise God gives to those who wait humbly for Him.

Peter begins this part of God's agreement by writing, "after you have suffered for a little while," God Himself will intervene. We need to address a pertinent question: Does Peter refer to heavenly reward or earthly blessing? Initially, it must again be emphasized one's ultimate reward rests in heaven. Tremendous disappointment awaits those who look for their heaven on earth. Paul taught the same precept, noting the difference between the temporal versus the eternal in Second Corinthians 4:17: "For momentary, light affliction is producing for us an eternal weight of glory far beyond all comparison." No matter how horrendous one's life may be, no one will be disappointed with heaven. Peter concurred, writing that the believer's reward is "reserved in heaven for you" (1:4). Further, Peter explained, "the proof of your faith, being more precious than gold which is perishable, even though tested by fire, may be found to result in praise and glory and honor at the revelation of Jesus Christ" (1:7). Also in the initial verse of the application section of First Peter, he wrote, "fix your hope completely on the grace to be brought to you at the revelation of Jesus Christ" (1:13). That our ultimate reward and deliverance await us in heaven should not undermine the enjoyment of life. God does bless our lives. However, if God blessed only in this life, it would be limited and temporary. Eternal glory, eternal reward, eternal face-to-face fellowship with God and the saints of the ages await. Earthly reward alone would hardly keep the interest of angels.

Although both the writings of Peter and Paul (and others) reveal believers will receive their ultimate reward in heaven, this does not mean First Peter 5:10 must also refer to future glory. We should consider a few factors. Initially, if Peter referred only to heaven, then in essence he counseled the sufferers to give up on this life. Such was not Peter's intent. However, a promise of guaranteed physical deliverance was not his intent either. As much as we do not like to think about it, martyrdom and "untimely deaths" are possibilities for believers. Not to be morbid with this, but believers who "die early" (no such term exists with God) arrive at their eternal home a little earlier than others do. We grieve for our loss, not theirs. The mourners need grace and strength, not those in God's presence. While the promises of First Peter 5:10 hold true for those who steadfastly endure suffering, we never box in or corner God. God is not a mathematical formula that works the same every time. He has different and unique plans for us, including when and how we will go home to be with Him. We should plan to have a long and fruitful life, but we are also to have our spiritual bags packed and be ready for either His arrival or our departure. We should look to enjoy the life God has given us. For those who suffer intensely not only is this difficult, at times it is humanly impossible. God must intervene if there is to be any joy in life, even as was true for Job. Also, Peter wrote specifically for those who faced suffering. Every believer ultimately will be "perfected, confirmed, strengthened, and established," once we get to heaven, including those who suffered greatly and those who did not. If First Peter 5:10 speaks only of heavenly reward, it would have no special relevance to suffering. These factors, plus the context and the vocabulary used, indicate Peter looked for God to work actively in this life. Heavenly reward will most certainly follow, and how one responds to suffering will affect one's eternal reward. Yet, heaven was not the pressing concern of the sufferers—living on earth was. In the four preceding verses Peter had exhorted the readers to humble themselves, casting all their anxiety on God, to resist Satan, be firm in their faith. It would be anticlimactic to dismiss their suffering with no hope of God's work until they arrived in heaven. Peter desired to motivate the readers to stand firm so they would see God display His intervention.

To give the readers assurance of God's action, Peter used four future tense verbs in 5:10 to explain what God would do for those who humbled themselves before Him. For emphasis Peter wrote no connecting links between the verbs, using short, rapid-fire items for what to expect. All the verbs have to do in some way with rebuilding or strengthening. This, too, points to God's work in our lifetime. We will one day receive a resurrected body that will not be "rebuilt," but new. Also, for one who has suffered relatively little, these promises may sound pleasant, but they are not the plea of one broken in spirit. Some faithful followers of Christ need little, if any, rebuilding. However, for those who have experienced the deeper ravages of suffering, strong hope of rebuilding that which is broken—including one's heart—is spiritually medicinal. Consequently, those who stand firmly in their suffering, actively incorporating the elements of 5:6-9 into their lives have four special assurances of God's work in their lifetime. Here is what you can expect God Himself to do at some time in the future.

The first act of God will be to "perfect" the sufferer. This word has the idea of fitting something together or arranging something properly. It has particular reference to an item in need of restoration, something needing to be made well or whole. It was the word used for fishermen mending their nets (Matt. 4:21), something of which Peter was quite familiar. One could also repair or "perfect" a vessel, such as a leaky boat. The word also referred to resetting a broken bone (Gal. 6:1). All these refer to something that is lacking or does not perform the way it was intended. Simply put, the first item God will perfect when He intervenes is to fix what is broken. For some, this would be rescue enough—but He is not finished yet; God has much more to accomplish.

However, before going any farther, we need to clarify one major consideration. While First Peter 5:10 presents four wonderful works God will do for faithful sufferers, we must guard against preconceptions of what God's rebuilding will entail. That God will perfect or rebuild does not necessarily mean that what currently causes your suffering will be taken from you. It may or may not—sometimes it cannot be. Physical restoration may not be any more expected in this life than the return of loved ones who have died. God does not say He will make things as before; He says He will intervene and rebuild. Whatever this means and however God chooses to perform this, you will by no means be disappointed. But how God achieves this is up to Him.

The next element of rebuilding God promises is to "confirm" the sufferers. The Greek word *steridzo* means "to set up, to fix firmly, to establish." Another nuance of this denotes "to strengthen with resolve." The word has to do with making something positionally solid, or to provide a support or buttress that is lacking. It depicts something wobbly and in risk of falling down unless properly undergirded. Such was even necessary for Jesus. Luke 9:51 reports, "And it came about, when the days were approaching for His Ascension, that He resolutely set [*steridzo*] His face to go to Jerusalem." Here, Jesus Himself resolved; it was divine self-determination. Again, Peter humbled himself by using His failure as an example to others. Jesus addressed this same word to him at the Last Supper. Having told Peter that Satan would sift him as wheat, Jesus said in Luke 22:32, "but I have prayed for you, that your faith may not fail; and you, when once you have turned again, strengthen [*steridzo*] your brothers." Peter remembered what it was like for him, and he passed on the same exhortation to his readers. He would never say, "I will strengthen you." He realized true strength originates from the Lord. First Peter 5:10 promises God will confirm or establish. God does not require us to exhibit the same resolve Jesus had—we never could. He calls us to submit; He will take care of the confirming and strengthening. When the confirming occurs you will know it is not your own strength but God's. After all, humbling yourself means putting yourself in a position where God can work. He will too. Stand firm.

The third word, "strengthen," is a little more difficult to compare with other uses because it occurs nowhere else in the New Testament. It conveys the sense of giving or imparting strength. Obviously God is never redundant. He intended a different nuance of meaning from the two previous words that also denote giving strength. Perhaps this was God's way "to leave Himself open" to show He will respond to whatever strength His faithful ones need. Perhaps it is as multifaceted as are the means of suffering. At first glance, these words seems almost an overkill for strengthen. God intended it so. He wanted the sufferer still in the midst of the fiery ordeal to anticipate with hope His intervention. The greater the weakness, the greater the strength needed. One word promising God's strengthening would suffice. Peter's threefold use of words conveying "strengthen" more than covers whatever need arises.

The final verb "establish" means "to give a firm foundation, to lay a firm foundation." Paul used the same word in Ephesians 3:17 when he prayed the believers would "be rooted and grounded in love." This word is similar to the second word "confirm," but there is a subtle difference. "Confirm" places emphasis on building up that which is weak or wobbly. "Establish" refers to the foundation on which something rests. Sometimes we wish God revealed more information in Scripture. Peter does not write this word for word, but it would make sense that Jesus Himself is that foundation. After all, in the previous verses Peter wrote about Satan prowling around seeking someone to destroy. Maybe someone who is "established" in the sense Peter used means God places him or her in a position where Satan can no longer do as he desires. The testing is complete; the approval of faith gained. I do not mean to stretch this, and again, biblical information is scarce. Neither does this mean a believer reaches the point where standing against Satan is unnecessary. Angels still maintain a cautious respect for Satan's power (Jude 9); we of the flesh must even more so. Yet, the Bible makes no other reference to Satan once God again placed the hedge back around Job. Likewise James, who always emphasized the believers' responsibility, wrote in James 4:7, "Submit therefore to God. Resist the devil and he will flee from you." Since James and First Peter write similarly about humbling oneself before God, but write from different vantage points, perhaps these connect. Left to Satan, even if we passed a particular test, he would devise some other brutal attack. The believer stands; God finally intervenes and confirms; Satan flees. Taking James and First Peter together, however, offers new insight into resisting Satan. Satan flees when God establishes us. Our resistance is one of the means God uses, but it is nonetheless His power working. Satan does not flee from God's angels who are immensely stronger than any mortal. Do we naively think he would flee from weak and stumbling mortals, such as you and I, based on our own effort or power? Resist Satan, and he will flee from you—but if you looked over your shoulder, spiritually speaking, you would see God's nearness to you is the reason he flees. This concept harmonizes with Peter's previous use of "establish." God, who could intervene at any time, does so after we have suffered "for a little while." He places us on the solid foundation of Himself, where Satan fears approaching. Even our best resistance is only a demonstration of God's strength, not our own. What a gracious hope He grants to believers. Stand firmly until He establishes.

If you are suffering, God has given you specific elements to expect. He Himself will perfect, confirm, strengthen, and establish us. All are words of rebuilding and making strong that which is not. It points to His strength, not one's self-effort. He gives us more than hope—He gives us Himself. Peter's exhortation in 5:12 calls us to exhibit faith in action: "I have written to you briefly, exhorting and testifying that this is the true grace of God. Stand firm in it!" We should—and we must. God gives the victory, but He chooses to rebuild and remake us in the process. Stand firm.

What overwhelming grace to know that our suffering is short and for a purpose, and that God Himself will intervene to rebuild. Add to this the growing weight of eternal reward, and it makes us almost—almost, but not quite—sorry for those who never have suffered greatly. Unknown to human reasons but all part of His grand design, God will bring you to a point where you can be a firsthand experiential witness of His magnificent work. What a promise! What a God! We will also compare notes throughout eternity with this aspect of God's work as well. It makes us understand those in Revelation 4:10 who cast their crowns before God's throne, realizing all glory and praise belong to Him. God protects us, keeping us from the full assault and temptation we could never bear. Jesus stepped into human history to endure what we could not, and then amazingly shares the results of His victory we could never collectively achieve. God gives us strength to endure our trials, even when we whine and are impatient and unthankful. To top it off, if we look only to Him and endure, He will reward us, both on earth and into eternity. What have we achieved? He has done it all. It makes a little better sense why Paul instructed the Philippians, "It has been graciously given unto you not only to believe in Him, but also to suffer for His sake." God works such mighty deeds through and around those tried by fire who stand firmly until the end. To summarize, what God's Word states about those who suffer according to God's will is this: We are headed for glory. We get our "preview of coming attractions" in the next chapter. And, oh, what glory it is!

Chapter Ten

The Glory

One of the benefits of in-depth Bible study is it changes you forever, that is, if you honestly seek God and His Word and attempt to live by His truths. Whenever you search deeply in God's Word, verses and subjects you have read all your life burst into new meaning. It is though the eyes of your soul have suddenly opened, and you wonder why you did not see such dazzling truths earlier. The disciples who walked on the road to Emmaus experienced this. The resurrected Jesus appeared to them, but they did not know who He was. After the two informed Jesus of the events of the crucifixion week, Jesus—as virtually always—responded in an unexpected manner. Luke 24:25-26 records Jesus mildly rebuking the two, saying, "O foolish men and slow of heart to believe in all that the prophets have spoken. Was it not necessary for the Christ to suffer these things and to enter into His glory?" Beginning with Moses and all the prophets, Jesus "explained to them the things concerning Himself in all the Scriptures" (24:27). After Jesus revealed Himself and departed, the two disciples exclaimed, "Were not our hearts burning within us while He was speaking to us on the road, while He was explaining the Scriptures to us?" It still happens today. Having our spiritual eyes opened and our minds enlightened with God's truth burns within us in a good sense. The living and abiding Word of the living and abiding God has no substitute. It is manna to all who partake of it, revealing the Bread of Life to those who hunger, ministering healing balm to those who suffer.

Because God's Word is eternal, new wonders always await being discovered. For me, this is the thrill of Bible study: mining out from God's written treasure chest. Several times people would approach me after a class or church service and say, "This is wonderful!" They were right. They were not saying I was wonderful. In reality, what they were saying is they had their souls fed. I knew of what they spoke—God fed my soul before He fed theirs.

One such item you may have repeatedly read but maybe never noticed is the number of times the writers of Scripture associated suffering with glory. References occur in many different places throughout the Bible. For instance, in the verses just cited concerning the road to Emmaus, Jesus had to point out the necessity of His sufferings as the means to enter His glory. Peter described himself in First Peter 5:1 as a "witness of the sufferings of Christ, and a partaker [from the Greek *koinonia*, "fellowship"] also of the glory that is to be revealed." Peter explained that the confused Old Testament prophets predicted "the sufferings of Christ and the glories to follow" (1:11). After his instruction to the readers not to be surprised at their fiery trials, he continued, "but to the degree that you share the sufferings of Christ, keep on rejoicing; so that also at the revelation of His glory, you may rejoice with exultation" (4:13). Even in the promise verse of our previous chapter, Peter linked the two: "After you have suffered for a little while, the God of all grace, who called you to His eternal glory in Christ, will Himself perfect, confirm, strengthen and establish you." Suffering and glory, repeatedly linked, but always in that order.

But exactly what is God's glory? We understand to a degree what comprises suffering, but glory is a different matter. The Bible frequently depicts glory as rightly belonging to God, as well as glory believers will receive in the future. Still, knowing God's glory exists is not the same as comprehending it. Like many topics in Scripture, God gives us only a partial revelation and limited information. He most likely restricts His revelation because it would make no sense to us until we are in His presence. Often the truths God reveals only lead to more questions, most of which cannot be fully answered until we go to be with the Lord. In response to the deeper questions of life, God gives us what He wants us to know and says in essence, "Trust Me" for the rest. We must—and we do.

As I begin this final chapter, I feel as Solomon must have felt at the dedication of the Temple. Second Chronicles 6:18 records Solomon praying, "But will God indeed dwell with mankind on the earth? Behold, heaven and the highest heaven cannot contain Thee; how much less this house which I have built." The same is true when writing about God's glory. All the mammoth earthly volumes ever written would not do justice in presenting God's glory, let alone one simple chapter in a book. The subject is simply too expansive to condense into a few sentences. For instance, the word "glory" occurs over three hundred times in Scripture. Add such derivations as "glorify" or "glorified" or similar terms, plus the accompanying verses that tell of glory and yet do not contain the word itself, and the number exceeds five hundred to a thousand. By far the most numerous examples ascribe glory as belonging to God. In fact, "glory" is actually one of the names of God. First Samuel 15:29 states, "And also the Glory of Israel will not change His mind." We continually observe an aspect of God's glory in His creation. Psalm 19:1 states, "The heavens are telling of [or "declaring"] the glory of God." We could cite hundreds more references with different emphases and nuances. As we have seen, Scripture also reveals one important aspect of glory that relates to us. God will give glory as a future aspect of the believers' reward, and as before, frequently associates it with suffering. We usually do not think of glory when we suffer, but God does—and that is all that matters. Since God graciously revealed several promises concerning the glory that emerges out of Christian suffering, we would be wise to pay close attention.

The Hebrew word for glory in the Old Testament depicts radiance or brightness. Consequently, the Bible contains much about certain figures or people who saw the glory of God, or stated better, beheld a most limited aspect of His glory. Always God restricts the view of His glory since His full glory would consume all universes. The radiant nature of God's glory corresponds with Paul's writing in Second Corinthians 4:17, "For momentary, light affliction is producing for us an eternal weight of glory far beyond all comparison." Again, one of the authors of Scripture faced the dilemma of describing heavenly truths by earthly comparisons; they simply do not evenly match. We usually do not think of glory in terms of how much it weighs. Paul may have because the Hebrew words "weight" and "glory" come from the same root word. The "weight of glory" could also relate to Paul's earlier description of Christian rewards. In First Corinthians 3:12 he contrasted believers' works consisting of either wood, hay, and straw or gold, silver, and precious stones. We characterize and value the latter three by their weight; the more they weigh, the greater their value. Paul indicated that properly responding to the afflictions of this lifetime accrues for believers a great weight of eternal glory. This will make more sense when we stand before the Lord, but the principle is easily seen. Not only does the Bible again connect suffering and glory, it even teaches enduring suffering for Christ produces glory for us. I would not be surprised if we stand before Jesus, realize what this verse fully teaches, and then regret opportunity lost.

To get a better understanding of God's glory, we return to one of the places where we began, namely, the Transfiguration. Luke 9:32 associates glory with this momentous event: "Now Peter and his companions had been overcome with sleep; but when they were fully awake, they saw His glory and the two men standing with Him." It was also the event that sparked James and John to ask Jesus that they may sit with Him in His glory. We need to dig a little deeper in the Word to see what God intended by this unique preview of glory at Christ's Transfiguration—glory ultimately promised for you and me.

Did you ever consider why God brought Moses and Elijah to the Transfiguration? Luke 9:31 offers an aspect of this answer in that they talked with Jesus "of His departure that He was about to accomplish at Jerusalem." God graciously brought two revered Old Testament saints to Jesus for such a conversation. Other than with His Father, with whom else could Jesus converse concerning His pending sacrifice? The worldly-minded disciples yet in the midst of seeking their own glory and rank would only distract Him. No suitable earthly figure would suffice, so God sent two saints to stand with Jesus temporarily. But why these two? Why not Abraham, the progenitor of the race and David, the prototype king? Why not faithful Joshua and Daniel, both of whom exhibited stellar obedience before the Lord? Isaiah and Ezekiel would be good choices since both wrote of beholding the glory of God. The two simplest answers are first, God is God; it is His story. He could bring whomever He desired and need not explain Himself to anyone. The second answer offered by some is in Moses and Elijah we see the Law and the Prophets represented, which was another way of referring to the entire Old Testament. Jesus placed importance on this. He taught the two disciples on the road to Emmaus about Himself from Moses and all the Prophets. Two Old Testament saints standing on the Mount of Transfiguration would further identify Him with the messianic prophecies.

Both answers for why Elijah and Moses were present have credence, but the account contains much more. Maybe we can gain some new insights, especially since God links glory with suffering. Let us examine the participants of the Transfiguration, and then relate them to the promises of God.

We begin with Moses. Moses stood on the Mount of Transfiguration not only because of his association with the Law but also because of an event in his life centuries earlier. After the Jews received the first giving of the Law, they ratified a covenant of obedience to God (Exodus 24). However, this willful obedience did not last long. During his communing with God, Moses did not return to the camp for many days. Several people of Israel hastily and wrongly assumed their leader had died. They coerced Aaron to make a golden calf for them to be their new god. God informed Moses of their actions and stated, "Now then let Me alone, that My anger may burn against them and that I may destroy them; and I will make of you a great nation" (Ex. 32:10). Moses "argued" with God, reminding Him of the unconditional and eternal Abrahamic Covenant promises that Israel would never perish. In other words, Moses responded, "You cannot do that, God"—which was exactly what God wanted Moses to say. God would not destroy Israel, but not because they did not deserve it. God would not annihilate the fledgling nation because He would be true to His word. The sin of the people moved Moses to great holy wrath resulting in the execution of 3,000 men for their idolatry. However, the love and humility of Moses are evident as well. In Exodus 32:32 Moses implored God, "But now, if Thou wilt, forgive their sin—and if not, please blot me out from Thy book which Thou hast written!" What an immense love for an obstinate and unappreciative people! Not many people would ask God to take away their eternal salvation and give it to someone else. Not that this is possible—God did not accept his offer—but if it were possible, our own list would be very short, if it had any names on it at all.

The next chapter, Exodus 33, offers insights relevant to the Transfiguration. Because of the golden calf incident, God would no longer reside in the midst of the people lest He destroy them (33:3). Although the people repented and mourned, God had spoken. Since God had previously displayed His presence visibly, the removal of this presence would be a strong object lesson to Israel. Thus Moses used to take a tent and pitch it some distance outside the confines of the camp, calling this "the tent of meeting" (33:7). Only Moses could enter the tent, and when he did so, the manifestation of God's glory would descend there. The people would see this and worship God. However, they gazed on only from a distance; Moses fellowshipped with God. Exodus 33:11 states, "Thus the Lord used to speak to Moses face to face, just as a man speaks to his friend." What an awe-inspiring concept—to talk with God face to face as a friend. What would you say? Would you ask Him anything? Would you make a request before Him?

Moses did. In Exodus 33:13 Moses requested, "Now therefore, I pray Thee, if I have found favor in Thy sight, let me know Thy ways, that I may know Thee, so that I may find favor in Thy sight." God encouraged Moses by responding in 33:17, "I will also do this thing of which you have spoken; for you have found favor in My sight, and I have known you by name." The cry of Moses' heart replied in return, "I pray Thee, show me Thy glory!" Moses had witnessed aspects of God's glory in the fire at Mount Sinai and the pillars of fire and the cloud. Yet, he realized God's glory consisted of so much more, and he made request to see it. In Exodus 33:19 God responded in a way which initially does not seem to match the request: "I Myself will make all goodness pass before you, and will proclaim the name of the Lord before you; and I will be gracious to whom I will be gracious, and will show compassion on whom I will show compassion." God's reply was not exactly what Moses expected in response to asking to see God's glory. The answer did, however, relate to his earlier request of knowing God's ways (33:13). Before Moses could reply, God continued, but "you cannot see My face, for no man can see Me and live!" However, God offered more.

> *Behold, there is a place by Me, and you shall stand there on the rock; and it will come about, while My glory is passing by, that I will put you in the cleft of the rock and cover you with My hand until I have passed by. Then I will take My hand away and you shall see My back, but My face shall not be seen.*

One of the intriguing items about this passage is that the Bible never described such an event after this. This does not mean that it did not occur. It is only that Moses wrote so much about the request and interaction with God, one would expect the same description when God displayed His glory. It is though Moses wrote a tremendous introduction to a sublime event, but the main act never transpires. It most likely occurred, at least in partial fulfillment, shortly thereafter. Exodus 34 indicates Moses' face shown from being in the presence of God. To some degree God showed Moses a refracted measure of His glory, and simply being near it caused Moses to glow with a heavenly aura visible to others. Yet to another degree, God did not grant Moses' request—at least not then.

We have met our first participant of the Transfiguration. We will tie in Moses' encounter with God after we meet our second witness of the Transfiguration, the prophet Elijah.

Elijah ministered when most people in the northern kingdom of Israel lived in rebellion before their God. The nation could trace much of their sinfulness to the influence of their leader then, wicked King Ahab. First Kings 16:30 offers this synopsis of his reign: "And Ahab, the son of Omri, did evil in the sight of the Lord more than all who were before him." Part of the reason for his evil activities was from his marriage to the evil woman Jezebel, who led Ahab "to serve Baal and worship him" (16:31). The two following verses list some of Ahab's sins against God:

> So he erected an altar for Baal in the house of Baal, which he built in Samaria. And Ahab also made the Asherah [a wooden symbol of a female god]. Thus Ahab did more to provoke the Lord God of Israel than all the kings of Israel who were before him. (16:32-33)

No doubt much of the nation followed Ahab and Jezebel's rebellion, especially since their idolatry encouraged sexual sins as part of the pagan worship.

In the midst of such flagrant apostasy God raised up the prophet Elijah, who stood against the sins of the king, becoming Ahab's perpetual nemesis. Elijah pronounced God's judgment that no rain or dew would fall on the land until his permissive word, and it came about precisely as he predicted. First Kings 18:1 notes the drought lasted three years, undoubtedly causing tremendous suffering and grief on the people. However, when Ahab encountered Elijah, Ahab blamed God's prophet for the afflictions, accusing, "Is this you, you troubler of Israel." Elijah countered with the truth, "I have not troubled Israel, but you and your father's house have, because you have forsaken the commandment of the Lord, and you have followed the Baals" (18:18). Since two gods existed in Israel, both claiming supremacy, the next logical step would be a contest between the two. The one who showed forth his power would be the true God of Israel. Having summoned the 450 false prophets of Baal against one man of God, Elijah set the issue before the people: "How long will you hesitate between two opinions? If the Lord is God, follow Him; but if Baal, follow him" (18:21). The verse adds, "But the people did not answer him a word." However, God always forces one to choose between Him and someone or something else. Remaining silent is simply another mode of disbelief, and God never tolerates silence concerning His identity.

Most of you know the account. If not, you can read the details in First Kings 18. From morning to noon and then beyond the false prophets called out to Baal. When Baal did not answer, the false prophets "cut themselves according to their custom with swords and lances until the blood gushed out on them" (1 Kings 18:28). Verse 29 summarizes the futility of their actions: "but there was no voice, no one answered, no one paid attention." After Elijah's prayer, God consumed his waterlogged sacrifice, as well as that of Baal, by sending fire from heaven. The fickle nation gasped, "The Lord, He is God; the Lord, He is God," perhaps speaking in the same repetitious manner they had learned from their incantations before Baal. However, now was not the time for teaching; it was time for action. Similar to Moses slaying those who led the worship of the golden calf, Elijah followed God's display of power by slaying the 450 false prophets of Baal.

Surprisingly, having boldly confronted the king, the nation, and the false prophets, and seeing God show His faithfulness, Elijah then cowered when threatened by Jezebel. After her false prophets had been slain, Jezebel threatened Elijah, saying, "So may the gods do to me and even more, if I do not make your life as the life of one of them by tomorrow about this time." How short a memory Elijah displayed—almost as short as our own memories of God's previous deliverances in our lives. Jezebel invoked the "gods," plural, who did not and could not answer just hours before at their own altar. A man of God should by no means consider threats based on an oath from impotent pagan gods as certain, especially when God Almighty remains his Leader and Protector. However, as is strangely true throughout both the Word and life, temporary stumbling and spiritual defeat often follow great spiritual victory. Elijah fled Jezebel in fear. Having gone to Beersheba, virtually the southern most point of Judah, Elijah then fled a day's journey into the wilderness—both a literal and spiritual wilderness. Elijah became so distraught he asked God to let him die. This is a rather unusual request since he fled Jezebel for fear she would kill him. If death were Elijah's true intent, he could have saved himself the trip.

Now comes God's intervention, as well as factors relevant to the Transfiguration. God sent not only an angel to minister and sustain Elijah, but also "the angel of the Lord" (1 Kings 19:7). This is not the place to delve into this intriguing Old Testament character in great detail. In its simplest terms, the angel of the Lord seems to be a preincarnate visit to the earth by Jesus. Jesus, who was born in Bethlehem, always existed as the second member of the Godhead. From time to time Jesus would step into His creation to accomplish a specific task. He was not merely an angel, but God the Son who took on this temporary form. After all, if the Son took "the form of a bondservant, being made in the likeness of men" (Phil. 2:7), it was no problem for Him to display Himself in a transitory likeness. Obviously, if Jesus came to earth demonstrating the full power of His glory, He would consume all His creation. He had to take on a vastly milder appearance in order to converse with certain biblical characters. The angel of the Lord made several appearances in the Old Testament. In fact, although most people do not realize this, it was the angel of the Lord who appeared to Moses in the burning bush (Ex. 3:2), whom the Bible also designates as God in verse 4. Added to this is the fact the angel of the Lord never appears again after the birth of Jesus. Because of these and other supports, quite a large number of Bible commentators identify the angel of the Lord as Jesus Christ.

So Elijah did not receive sustenance from one member of God's angelic host; the despondent prophet received nourishment from Jesus Himself. Similar to the disciples eating broiled fish the resurrected Jesus prepared for them, the Lord also fed Elijah. The Bread of Life and the Giver of living waters provided the weary prophet bread cakes and a jar of water. Elijah's dejection was so great, no mention is made of him being in awe or amazement at the angel of the Lord's presence. Elijah might not have even realized he stood before the very presence of God. Also, as is true for many of us, his despair might have been so great he did not recognize or appreciate God's sustenance during his misery. Yet, God appeared to Elijah to bring him through this defeat, not to destroy the man. The angel of the Lord strengthened Elijah and then sent him on a forty-day journey to Mount Horeb, also known as Mount Sinai, the same place Moses had encountered God when he received the Law.

Many who study this account have a difficult time understanding Elijah's situation. The encounter with the false prophets was a victory, not a defeat. His side—God's side—won, not lost. Although not specifically stated in Scripture, a tremendous spiritual battle must have been transpiring within Elijah. The rampant idolatry of Baal and the Asherah gives evidence of strong demonic activity. In First Corinthians 10:20 Paul informed the ignorant Corinthians that when one sacrificed to an idol, it was in reality a sacrifice to a demon. Idolatry proliferated most of Israel, from the king down to the lowly servant. Simply put, God's own people in their promised land lived within a demonic stronghold. A second deduction, although not stated verbatim in Scripture, relates to Elijah's strategic role. If you were Satan, and your stronghold was being disassembled, your false prophets destroyed, and the people marginally began to turn back to God, would you not do all within your power to defeat your human antagonist? Most likely what happened was Satan sifted Elijah as he later would one day sift Peter. Discouraged and defeated in spirit, Elijah despaired for his own life. If Peter and Elijah could have sat down within eyesight of each other, each showing the spiritual scars of their souls' sifting, they would readily recognize the source of the wounds inflicted on each other.

God confronted Elijah in a cave and instructed him, "Go forth, and stand on the mountain before the Lord." This differs from the earlier episode with Moses in that Moses requested to see God's glory. Elijah made no such request. God understood this and responded by giving small exhibitions of His power. Similar to what God promised Moses, First Kings 19:11 records, "And behold, the Lord was passing by!" In human terms a wind strong enough to rip apart rocks and mountains, a great earthquake, and a consuming fire would cause most people to marvel before God, to quake in fear at His power. Yet by God's terms, when one considers the unfathomable expanse of His creation—and the expanse of His glory—His display limited to a small area surrounding Mount Horeb required no great effort. It pales in significance to God's creation of the earth, moon, or stars, or even the pinnacle of His creation, namely, you and me. So God demonstrated only a microscopic amount of His power before Elijah, but it was an object lesson the despondent prophet needed at that time. Any of the three displays were vastly superior to the "power" of the silent gods at the pagan altar. Any of the three displays would easily destroy the pagan queen Jezebel, or any other adversary, if God had so intended.

So while the backside glory of God passed by Moses, only an echo display of God's power passed by Elijah. Elijah did not view God; he viewed the effects of God's presence—and there is an important difference. Scripture makes this emphatic distinction by noting, "but the Lord was not in the wind," "but the Lord was not in the earthquake," "but the Lord was not in the fire" (1 Kings 19:11). Elijah witnessed power temporarily displayed by God in a small degree, but not face-to-face fellowship, and not a display of God's glory.

We have met the two Old Testament characters who will attend the Transfiguration. We will now walk a little with Peter, James, and John in the steps leading to this momentous event.

Matthew 16 tells of Jesus and His disciples traveling through Caesarea Philippi, in the district of Panias. Their geographical location had much to do with Jesus' forthcoming questions to them. The Greeks named the region for the Greek mythological god Pan, a half-goat, half-man being. Pagan shrines to Pan and other gods remain until this day, easily visible to visitors to Caesarea Philippi. The first Herod, ever the politician and never the loyalist to God, built a temple to Rome and Augustus Caesar. Thus, the previous world empire Greece and the current one Rome both had pagan artifacts dedicated to the worship of their multiple false gods. Jesus and the disciples no doubt had viewed these as well. Perhaps even within sight of the pagan shrines carved into the mountain, or standing among the shrines to the false gods, Jesus began asking His disciples, "Who do people say the Son of Man is?" Public opinion and false summations were not His true concern. Jesus was leading the disciples to the core question He really desired to ask.

The response by the disciples demonstrates the wide public interest and debate Jesus had aroused. Accordingly, answers about His origin differed. Many viewed Him through their superstitions and erroneous beliefs. They knew Jesus was different; they just were not sure who or what He was. Luke's parallel account shows the disciples answering that some people concluded that Jesus was "John the Baptist, and others Elijah, but others, that one of the prophets of old has risen again." The disciples offered answers only from Jewish sources. At this point in their lives they were loath to interact with Gentiles. The answers by the masses are interesting assessments in that each of the three answers was in some way connected with death. Herod had only recently executed John the Baptist, Elijah escaped death by being transported to heaven, and the other prophets had all died. The works Jesus did, let alone His divine words, caused the people to elevate their estimation of Him beyond the present world. However, the majority could not conceive He had come down out of heaven as a divine Being.

The world's assessment of Him at this time was not Jesus' concern—the twelve were. The backdrop of Greek and Roman false gods coupled with the misconceptions of the Jews only added to the mystery of this Man. Jesus asked His disciples—and everyone who will ever live—the great question of all eternity: "Who do you say that I am?" Simon Peter, human leader of the apostles, answered, "Thou art the Christ, the Son of the living God." It was not his answer entirely. Such was the importance of the answer God Himself saw fit to reveal it to Peter. This was not the first such revelation from the Father concerning Jesus. From the Old Testament prophets through the enunciation to Mary and the revelatory dream to Joseph, God bore witness that Jesus was His Son. God sent angels to announce Jesus' birth. At Jesus' baptism God spoke from heaven, "This is My beloved Son [literally, "My Son, the Beloved"], in whom I am well pleased." The Bible does not reveal whether any of the disciples were present at Jesus' baptism, but they would know about the voice from heaven, especially those who initially were disciples of John the Baptist, who frequently spoke of the Coming One. God desired Peter's response concerning Jesus' identity to be so certain that He answered it Himself by revealing it to Peter.

Considering other factors, God made quite a statement through Peter. Only weeks earlier, after Jesus walked on water, the disciples received Jesus into the boat. In natural response they worshiped Him and said, "You are certainly God's Son!" While this is better than what the masses said about Jesus, it was nonetheless incomplete. The disciples used no article in front of their attestation of Jesus. They did not say, "You are the Son of God." Instead, they said what could be translated, "Truly God's Son you are," or "Truly, a Son of God, you are." As Nicodemus had testified earlier, they knew God was with Jesus. They knew the Messiah would be born.

They had a difficult time harmonizing all this with "Hear, O Israel the Lord is God, the Lord is One." Their concept of Messiah was that He would be human, as He was. That He could simultaneously be divine confused them, as it would likewise confuse the Pharisees. Not too long after this account, in Matthew 22:42 Jesus demolished the Pharisees' entire system of religious thought with one simple question. Jesus asked, "Whose son is the Christ?" The Pharisees retorted, "David's Son," no doubt humiliated that they received such a simple question any Jewish child could answer. They all knew God made a covenant with David that would ultimately bring forth the Messiah. Jesus countered with another simple question, "Why then does David in the Spirit call Him Lord?" The Messiah would be human and son, but He was also Lord. In fact, He was already Lord one thousand years earlier when David penned the Psalm—and one thousand years before the birth of Jesus. The Pharisees dared not reply; neither do many modern skeptics who honestly examine the claims of Messiah.

For a Jew to equate someone as having the same essence as Yahweh was either a true statement of worship or a defiantly blasphemous one. There was no middle ground. The disciples knew Israel could collectively be considered the children of God, but one among them as the unique Son of God, they would not naturally say. While in the boat the disciples progressed closer to the truth about Jesus, but they still had not yet arrived. At Caesarea Philippi, God intervened. This time Peter proclaimed, literally in the Greek, "You are *the* Christ, *the* Son of *the* God *the* living One." Not one of many false gods, not an immortalized Hebrew prophet, not a spurious superstition erroneously linked to another's identity. Jesus stands alone. It had taken about three years for the disciples to arrive at this declaration, but God had not rushed them. It was important that they know, which is a step beyond simple belief. Peter did not say, "I think you are the Christ," or "I believe you are the Christ." This alone would not suffice. Belief can change; faith can waver. Before His death, John the Baptist, who baptized Jesus and heard God's very own voice from heaven, who decades earlier had leaped in his mother's womb in the mere presence of the unborn Jesus, had his belief stretched to its breaking point. While himself imprisoned and facing imminent death, he sent his disciples to ask Jesus, "Are you the Coming One, or should we look for someone else?" "The Coming One" was a Jewish term for Messiah. If you had asked

John the Baptist at that time who Jesus was, he would most likely have hesitated before responding. John did not renounce Jesus, but his circumstances caused him to waver in uncertainty; things had not worked out as John had believed they would. Belief remains necessary—divine revelation is vastly more substantial. Heaven and earth will pass away before any of God's Word will. What Peter spoke was God's word—Peter was simply the vessel. With God's help, Peter knew.

Instead of instructing the twelve to shout this revelation on the very mountaintops that surrounded them, Jesus warned them to tell no one that He was the Christ (Matt. 16:20). It had taken approximately three years of living with Jesus, witnessing the mighty and matchless works and words of God daily for Peter to state—under divine inspiration—Jesus was the Christ, the Son of God. How much longer would it take for those entrapped by fearful superstition, perhaps inwardly receptive to surrounding pagan deities, to arrive at the same conclusion? How spiritually clouded the average Jew had become because of the lifeless rituals espoused by the Pharisees and Sadducees, let alone the blatant corruption of the high priesthood of Annas and Caiaphas. His disciples would one day tell the world—but now was not the time. Being in full control of all events, Jesus did not want to stir up the Jewish authorities into action before all things were in place, including a year's more instruction for His apostles. Jesus Himself would bear witness before the nation's leaders—both Jewish and Gentile—on the night of His trial. That would be the appropriate time. For now the disciples had to keep their conversation among themselves. Jesus knew they had much, much more to learn and sift through their minds. Besides, a traitor walked among them who did not believe Jesus was the Christ, the Son of the living God.

Peter's declaration opened the way for greater revelation, some of which they could not readily receive. Matthew 16:21 states, "From that time Jesus Christ"—Matthew himself adding his own written testimony that Jesus was the Christ, the Son of the living God. Usually Matthew simply wrote, for instance, "Jesus went out." This was the first time Matthew referred to Him in his Gospel as Jesus Christ since the two introductory verses in Matthew 1:1 and 1:18. "From that time Jesus Christ began to show His disciples that He must go to Jerusalem, and suffer many things from the elders and chief priests and scribes, and be killed, and be raised up on the third day." Interestingly, here Jesus attributed His death to the Jews, not the Romans. He would later add the means would be crucifixion, the Roman manner of execution. Regardless of the manner of death, this revelation did not match the disciples' perception of the Son of God or the promised reign of Messiah. In fact, if this had come before the revelation from God through Peter, it would have tremendously weakened their faith. Perhaps some would have even fallen away. A good time would never exist for such dire predictions, but it was necessary both for Jesus' work as well as for training His disciples. Peter responded as Simon, perhaps proudly assuming he could speak for God, having just done so a few moments before. Jesus was the Christ, the Son of the Living God, but at this point of his life Peter was still giving instructions to Him, still attempting to direct and inform Jesus. When Peter tried to prohibit Jesus from facing the death He had just predicted, Jesus would not tolerate it, speaking a stilting rebuke to Peter.

The Apostles must have swooned from these seemingly contradictory revelations. Jesus—who cast out demons by His command, stilled the tempest sea with a word, never once gave into Satan's attacks, raised the dead, continually baffled His opponents—would die? Who could kill Him? How could anyone kill Him? Not only that, but Jesus was God's Son. Who is brazen enough to harm the Son, the Beloved? Who is strong enough to take God's Son away from the Father? And what about the promised kingdom? The Bible presents hundreds of Old Testament prophecies of the kingdom coming in worldwide power and glory, with the Messiah reigning on David's throne. A defeated Messiah? A dead Messiah? The more they thought, the more their confusion intensified. Not only would Jesus die, but also those who followed Him would share a similar fate. In Matthew 16:24-25 Jesus informed them, "If anyone wishes to come after Me, let him deny himself, and take up his cross, and follow Me. For whoever wishes to save his life shall lose it; but whoever loses his life for My sake shall find it." How could this be? This was not what Jesus had previously taught them nor did it meet their expectations. Instead of the disciples escorting Jesus into glory, Jesus called anyone who wished to come after Him—and that includes us—to deny himself, take up his cross, and follow Him. Take up his cross? A cross was the means of death, not life, and a most grotesque death at that.

The disciples might have silently thought, "Jesus would be killed by the Jewish authorities, but crosses await us"—which meant a Roman execution. Rome tolerated defeated nations their religions, but they had no hesitation in executing insurrectionists. If such were their thoughts, Jesus confused them further by speaking of the future in diametrically different terms. Jesus, ever the Master Teacher, discerning their inward distress either through their audible gasps or else by His divine understanding, addressed their fears. He knew they would not understand at the present time, but one day they would. While it was true the Son of Man would die, He would return in glory. Jesus promised in Matthew 16:27: "For the Son of Man is going to come in the glory of His Father with His angels, and will then recompense every man according to his deeds." Luke 9:26-27 adds additional details, "For whoever is ashamed of Me and My words, of him will the Son of Man be ashamed when He comes in His glory, and the glory of the Father and of the holy angels." This is the first time recorded in Scripture where Jesus taught His apostles about the glory of God—especially the glory of God and how it related to Jesus.

It would be interesting to know Judas' thought and reaction to what Jesus had just revealed. Judas saw no glory, nor any hope for glory. At this point the glory of Jesus was only a matter of faith, not sight—but that would soon change for three of them. Mark's parallel account in 9:1 notes, "And He was saying to them [imperfect tense, "repeatedly said," or "began saying"], 'Truly I say to you, there are some who are standing here who shall not taste death until they see the kingdom of God after it has come with power.'"

The Bible does not disclose whether any of the disciples volunteered or asked to be one of the witnesses. Perhaps Jesus' multifaceted revelations simply overwhelmed them too much for them to say much of anything. They had so much they needed to sort through, so much new teaching which they could not rationally harmonize. During the past few days Jesus presented His first revelation that He would found His church, but He also predicted His death. The disciples received this, and for the most part believed it, but they were far from understanding it. Jesus was God's Son, the Christ, yet death awaited Him. They, too, were to lose their lives, take up their crosses and follow Him. We sometimes or generally associate "take up thy cross" as putting up with the difficulties and trials of life, and some even sing songs based on this phrase. To those earliest disciples, the phrase would be the equivalent of "Take up thy electric chair and follow Him." This was a call to death—not to life—and it was by no means a pleasant thought. Yet despite such predictions of tragedy, Jesus said He would return and judge the entire world. Not only that but He also promised to return in kingdom glory with kingdom power. In fact, some of the very ones who heard these words would witness this in their lifetime.

———————

The Transfiguration followed about a week after the events of Matthew 16—and what a week it had been! Disclosed within a seven-day period was Jesus' first prophecy about the church He Himself would build, the first specific prophecy of His pending crucifixion and resurrection, as well as the promised return of the King and His Kingdom. And as a pinnacle to all this, this section contains the first teaching by Jesus concerning His glory. Surprisingly Jesus had referred to God's glory very sparingly before. He would teach much more about it, but virtually all His teaching about the glory of God comes after the Transfiguration. Only once does Scripture contain a teaching about God's glory before the Transfiguration. Earlier Jesus rebuked the unbelieving Jews in John 5:41-44, saying,

> *"I do not receive glory from men; but I know you, that you do not have the love of God in yourselves. I have come in My Father's name, and you do not receive Me; if another shall come in his own name, you will receive him. How can you believe, when you receive glory from one another, and you do not seek the glory that is from the one and only God?"*

Now Jesus took the teaching deeper; now He associated the glory of God with Himself and with His reign—and He did so beginning at the Transfiguration. The Transfiguration served not only as a confirming sign to Peter's Holy Spirit-inspired declaration of Matthew 16:16, but also as a preview of the glory that would one day be manifested to the entire world. Jesus will return to earth "in His glory, and the glory of the Father and of the holy angels" (Luke 9:26; also Matt. 16:27; Mark 8:38). The three Gospel accounts each preview and connect the Transfiguration with Jesus' revelation concerning His glory.

Jesus selected Peter, James, and John to accompany Him, the Old Testament number required for witnesses of serious charges or attestations (Deut. 17:6). Luke 9:28 reveals that Jesus took the three as He went to pray, which might not have been anything unusual. Because of this, the other disciples most likely would not take special notice when the four departed. However, it was to be a most monumental time with their Lord as God Himself allowed these three simple Galilean fishermen a preview of the kingdom glory and power no one had ever witnessed before. Luke 9:29 states, "And while He was praying, the appearance of His face became different, and His clothing became white and gleaming" or literally, "flashing like lightning." Matthew 17:2 notes, "His face shone like the sun, and His garments became as white as light." Mark described it as "His garments became exceedingly white, ["sparkling"] as no launderer of earth can whiten them."

If that was not impressive enough for the three, "Behold, Moses and Elijah appeared to them, talking with Him." Luke 9:31 described Moses and Elijah as appearing in splendor, literally "in glory." Had it been any other time, Peter, James, and John witnessing the appearance of two Old Testament heroes would have been the most colossal event of their lives. Now, however, even Moses and Elijah paled in comparison. Jesus alone was the focus—Jesus alone showed forth glory. While Moses and Elijah shown, their glory was merely a reflection of His, much the same way Moses shown after talking face-to-face with God in Exodus 34. The three received the brief preview of glory God intended, but at that time they would not see His full glory. Luke 9:32 explains, "Now Peter and his companions had been overcome with sleep." This was not their fault but rather God's design. God similarly had Adam sleep so Eve could be created, and later Abraham sleep so God alone could ratify the Abrahamic Covenant. Peter, James, and John had to sleep as well, otherwise being in the midst of Jesus' overwhelming glory at the very least would have caused them to glow much in the same way Moses did in Exodus. Three power-seeking disciples could not have endured having such glory residing on them; it would be too much for them to withstand without continually boasting to the others. God made them sleep, but He awoke them in time to get one final glimpse of Jesus' glory. They knew it was His glory, and His alone. Moses and Elijah were key but secondary figures. Luke 9:32 shows this by noting the three "saw His glory"—not their glory—"and the two men standing with Him."

Peter spoke for the three saying it was good for them to be there and that he would build tabernacles for them all. God once more intervened and interrupted Peter. Matthew 17:5 states, "While he was still speaking, behold, a bright cloud overshadowed them." Luke reports, "They were afraid as they entered the cloud." If Moses had still been in his earthly body, he would not have feared—He had been in the cloud with God before from Exodus through Deuteronomy. God Himself revealed from the cloud in audible voice virtually the same pronouncement Peter had spoken days before. "This is My beloved Son, My Chosen One [Luke 9:35], with whom I am well-pleased. Listen to Him!" The three disciples fell face down in terrified dread as the cloud consumed them—only to find that Jesus came and touched them. They looked around and saw Jesus standing alone. In the Old Testament, when the nation lost the Ark of the Covenant to the Philistines, the people mourned because the glory of God had departed. In this case, the glory of God had not departed—it simply was contained again within the human confines of the Sacrificial Lamb. The glory was still there; Jesus could manifest it at any time if He had so desired—even in the midst of His scourging or crucifixion. Peter, James, and John had witnessed merely a sample of what will later be revealed in its totality. Presently, however, was not the time for the glory to be revealed. Now was the time for the descent down the mountain, and ultimately the descent down into death as well.

But the account in Luke 9 adds significant details not recorded in the other accounts. For instance, Luke 9:31 reveals that Moses and Elijah "were speaking [with Jesus] of His departure which He was about to accomplish at Jerusalem." The word departure is the Greek word *exodus* (the same word for the Exodus of the Bible), which is not the normal word used for death. The exodus of Jesus would not point so much to His death—although death was a major facet of this—but also to His burial, resurrection, and here, particularly to His ascension. The two prophets of God were speaking with Him, the Greek text employing an imperfect tense, noting somewhat of a protracted activity. It was a sustained conversation; not a rushed one. How striking that what Peter had attempted to prevent in Matthew 16 only a few days before became the focal point of the conversation for the Lamb and His two holy messengers.

Luke records Moses and Elijah were speaking of the departure Jesus was about to accomplish at Jerusalem. While some view this as the two prophets instructing Jesus about what lay ahead concerning His cross, this does not seem to be the case. Jesus had previously predicted His death, burial, and resurrection. He knew what awaited Him; He knew what He must do. The three earthly witnesses fell asleep, so we do not have any more details of their conversation. Yet along with their discourse and among other matters, Moses and Elijah might have been a visible reminder for Jesus. Even these two special agents of God needed the unblemished Lamb's blood just as much as Peter, James, and John. Though Moses had died and God had already transported Elijah to heaven, divine redemption had not yet occurred, not in the fullest sense anyway. But it would soon—in Jerusalem. Paul later wrote in Romans 3:23-26:

> For all have sinned and fall short of the glory of God, being justified by His grace through the redemption which is in Christ Jesus; whom God displayed publicly as a propitiation [covering] in His blood through faith. This was to demonstrate His righteousness because in the forbearance of God He passed over the sins previously committed; for the demonstration, I say, of His righteousness at the present time, that He might be just and the justifier of the one who has faith in Jesus.

Moses and Elijah—plus every Old Testament saint from Adam onward—needed a Redeemer. Without the appropriate propitiation, God must hold them accountable for the totality of their own sins—and no one of the human race would ever have fellowship with God throughout eternity. Without the atonement there would be no salvation; hell would await everyone born, life being only a daily trek closer to damnation. Moses and Elijah would not instruct Jesus concerning His sacrificial death; if anything they would thank Him in advance.

So why did God bring these five men to the holy mountain to be with Jesus? As before part of the answer is God is God; He does as He desires. However, along with the previous mention of Moses and Elijah representing the Law and the Prophets, we can find other reasons. For Moses, it was a more complete keeping of God's promise not only "to show me Thy glory!" but also God's promise of Exodus 33:19: "I Myself will make all goodness pass before you, and will proclaim the name of the Lord before you." He, too, beheld the glory of God in the Person of Jesus. The "all goodness" that passed before him came encased in Jesus—as He actually had throughout the Old Testament—and Moses heard God proclaim His name before him. For the discouraged prophet Elijah, God had previously demonstrated three elements of power, each time noting He was not within the power displayed. Having shown Elijah what He was not, God now revealed to him who He was in glory. Perhaps Elijah recognized Him as the Angel of the Lord who ministered to him centuries before. God was not present in the display of power that passed by Elijah, but He was present in the preview power of the King and His coming kingdom. Paul understood this as well. In First Corinthians 1:24 Paul described Jesus as "the power of God and the wisdom of God." Moses saw the glory; Elijah saw a projection of power—but God revealed both in the Person of Jesus.

Peter, James, and John likewise would never view Jesus the same again—or anything else regarding this world. For the remainder of their lives, the preview glory never departed from them. Over thirty years later, when Peter wrote his "death row epistle" of Second Peter, the Holy Spirit prompted him to return to that day when he beheld the glory of Jesus. Peter does not bemoan his approaching death; the longer he walked with the Lord, the more he placed the focus properly on the Lord he so deeply loved. In Second Peter 1:12-14 he informed his readers:

> *Therefore, I shall always be ready to remind you of these things, even though you already know them, and have been established in the truth which is present with you. And I consider it right, as long as I am in this earthly dwelling, to stir you up by way of reminder, knowing that the laying aside of my earthly dwelling is imminent, as also our Lord Jesus Christ has made clear to me.*

Ever the disciple, ever the learner, Peter wrote of his own death using the identical word Luke did of Jesus at the Transfiguration. "And I will also be diligent that at any time after my departure [literally, "my exodus"] you may be able to call these things to mind" (2 Pet. 1:15). As in Luke 9:31, Peter did not focus on his pending death—the crucifixion Jesus had previously revealed in John 21:18-19. When he wrote his final epistle, Peter did not tell of the cross, the nails, the torture, the thirst. He spoke of his exodus—and his entrance. A few verses earlier he wrote, "for in this way the entrance into the eternal kingdom of our Lord and Savior Jesus Christ will be abundantly supplied to you (2 Peter 1:11). The Greek word for "entrance" is built on the same word for "exodus," only with a different preposition attached to the front. Peter looked for both: the exodus and the entrance [*eisodus*].

Peter would leave this earthly abode, but by no means was he going out of existence. He was going home—and home to glory. He knew this already—He had witnessed the glory decades before. Notice how Peter connects the reference to his death with a reminder of the transfigurational glory he had once beheld, connecting the thoughts with the introductory word "for":

> For we did not follow cleverly devised tales when we made known to you the power and coming of the Lord Jesus Christ, but we were eyewitnesses of His majesty. For when He received honor and glory from God the Father, such an utterance as this was made to Him by the Majestic Glory, 'This is My beloved Son with whom I am well-pleased.'—and we ourselves heard this utterance made from heaven when we were with Him on the holy mountain (2 Peter 1:16-18).

The effects of witnessing the Transfiguration likewise never left John. Many years after this divine encounter the aged apostle wrote, "And the Word became flesh, and dwelt among us, and we beheld His glory, glory as the only begotten from the Father, full of grace and truth." John remembered—and John looked back. The glory of God was a progressive study—and a progressive hope—as Jesus walked them through spiritual truths He alone prepared them to receive. John could not look at the life of Jesus without reference to His glory. Even the first miracle Jesus performed, in turning the water to wine at the wedding in Cana, the elder John noted the significance of this divine work by highlighting, "This beginning of the signs Jesus did in Cana of Galilee, and manifested His glory, and His disciples believed in Him" (John 2:11). Small, defracted glimpses of His glory, John knew now, but glory nonetheless. A greater glory resided as evident at the Transfiguration—and as evident in the glorified Jesus whom John beheld—and whom John worshiped—in Revelation 1.

How much more meaningful, then, becomes what John—and even more so, the Holy Spirit—revealed about the greatness of our salvation in Christ. First John 3:1 encourages Christ's own with this foundational, awe-evoking truth: "See how great a love the Father has bestowed upon us, that we should be called children of God; and such we are. For this reason the world does not know us, because it did not know Him." John continued in

3:2, "Beloved, now we are children of God, and it has not yet appeared what we shall be. We know ["to know intellectually; to understand"] that when He appears, we shall be like Him, because we shall see Him just as He is." Remember this is written from the viewpoint of an eyewitness of the glory of God in the face of Jesus—and John reveals to us that we shall be like Him. We will not only marvel at His glory, by God's grand design, we will likewise be partakers:

> *But, we should always give thanks to God for you, brethren beloved by the Lord, because God has chosen you from the beginning for salvation through sanctification by the Spirit and faith in the truth. And it was for this He called you through our gospel, that you may gain the glory of our Lord Jesus Christ*
> (2 Thess. 2:13-14).

Moses and Elijah glowed from being in Christ's presence. We will too, only fully, expanded, and on into eternity, since we will reign with Him forever—and be like Him.

The third human witness, James, would most likely have written about the glory also, except Herod executed him before he ever did (Acts 12:1-2). He most likely would have followed the example of his two companions and spoke freely that he beheld the glory of Jesus. Glory. Power. Majesty. Honor. All demonstrated in Jesus—all due Him. Once witnessed no earthly or angelic glory ever comes close. In fact, no true glory exists other than the glory of God.

Together the five witnesses saw the glory and power of God, each originating from a background contrasting who or what God is not. Moses' request to see God's glory followed the idolatry of the golden calf. Elijah saw the effects of the wind, the earthquake, and the fire after his victory over the false prophets of Baal. Peter, James, and John beheld his glory only miles away from the false gods of Caesarea Philippi and the Jews' erroneous conclusions about Jesus. Although prohibited from doing so at the time, later the three could respond to those who thought Jesus was Elijah. This was part of the answer to Jesus' initial spark question of "Who do people say the Son of Man is?" (Matt. 16:13). Although many would not believe them, the three could respond, "No, Jesus is not Elijah. We have seen them both standing in glory, but it was only the glory of the Son. We heard the Father say of only One, 'He is My beloved Son, My chosen One, in whom I am well pleased.' He is the Christ, the Son of the Living God— and He will return in His glory—and in the glory of the Father and the holy angels."

———————

One other derivative of in-depth Bible study is that you often come away envious of those who were present with Jesus. What things God permitted them to hear! To see! To experience! Jesus recognized this, informing the disciples of their most privileged position, stating, "For truly I say to you, that many prophets and righteous men desired to see what you see, and did not see it; and to hear what you hear, and did not hear it" (Matt. 13:17). On human terms it seems almost unfair that we should not be allowed to view the same glory. Yet, Scripture does connect us with the glory of Jesus, and as before, links it with suffering.

In Romans 8:15-18 Paul instructed his readers regarding suffering and the future glory. "For you have not received a spirit of slavery leading to fear again, but you have received a spirit of adoption as sons by which we cry out, 'Abba, Father!'"—the same Abba Jesus cried out to in the Garden.

> *"The Spirit Himself bears witness with our spirit that we are children of God, and if children, heirs also, heirs of God and fellow-heirs with Christ, if indeed we suffer with Him in order that we may also be glorified with Him. For I consider that the sufferings of this present time are not worthy to be compared with the glory that is to be revealed to us."*

Paul knew precisely of what he wrote. He, too, received a preview of glory when he was caught up to heaven (2 Cor. 12:1-4). This same glory awaits you, if you believe the Cup, the Road, the Gift, the Fellowship, the Surprise, and the Blessing are all worth it. Abba, suffering and glory—just as Christ partook.

———————

One morning I walked along the stately campus of Southeastern Baptist Seminary, a few minutes before I had to teach a class. It was a cold January morning, before sunup, a little over four months since the devastation of Hurricane Fran. Southeastern is an old campus. Some of the massive oaks have lived there for over a century. Wonderful, monumental trees of God's design, some reaching over six feet in diameter at their base, adorned the campus with a beauty unequaled by any human creation. I had walked the campus quite often both before and after the hurricane and knew the storm had caused considerable damage to the campus. It was disturbing to see where the trees had once lived. During the hurricane dozens of the larger trees had blown over, leaving rootballs of mud extending over ten feet high. Pictures of these overturned natural monuments made our local newspaper. While other trees survived, the campus looked markedly different. It looked sadly bare. Decades would pass before the campus looked the same again—if it ever did. With a wisp of melancholy I contemplated the void left by the missing trees. In the midst of my musings, the sun peaked over the horizon with the pristine beauty reserved for a winter sunrise. Arthritis has affected my eyes, and I actually feel when light hits it, as it did that moment. Along with the physical light, I felt as though God had also turned on another light inside me. While it is true the trees were gone and would not return, from where I was standing, their removal gave a better view of the glory of God's sunrise as I had never before witnessed. I would not purposefully have removed those trees to get a better view; it was merely a refracted blessing coming out of the loss. I could see better, farther, appreciate the glory of the sunrise, more than I ever could from that same vantage point only months before.

Suffering produces much the same effect on a spiritual level, if you allow God free rein in your life. Those who suffer usually have lost something or someone dear to them. The loss may be the use of one's body in ways previously enjoyed, or the loss may be the removal of someone they love. It was not their choice to suffer any more than it was for the trees to be blown over during the hurricane. As painful as it is, suffering can produce one unique effect: It can give us a better vantage of God's approaching glory than we had before. Our view of anticipated glory is not so much the glory of a physical sunrise, but the approaching glory of the Lord Jesus Christ. In Revelation 22:16, the aged Apostle John records Jesus declaring,

> *"I, Jesus, have sent My angel to testify to you these things for the churches. I am the root and the offspring of David, the bright morning star."* [The response to this promise in the next verse

is a natural one, a hunger for those who hurt, a cry from a heart crushed by suffering:] *"And the Spirit and the Bride say, 'Come.' And let the one who hears say, 'Come.' And let the one who is thirsty come; let the one who wishes take the water of life without cost."*

Suffering can produce a yearning for the Bright Morning Star. Suffering tends to make us look to others for help and support—Jesus desires a large part of such looking to be directed toward Him. As Peter admonished his readers, "Fix your hope completely on the grace to be brought to you at the revelation ["uncovering"] of Jesus." He remains faithful. Stand firm.

In Revelation 21:1-2, John recorded that he saw a new heaven and a new earth coming down from heaven to replace the present one. When this occurs, we will receive something else from God. Revelation 21:3-5 records God promising,

> *"Behold, the tabernacle of God is among men, and He shall dwell among them, and they shall be His people, and God Himself* [the same God Himself of First Peter 5:10, used again for emphasis] *shall be among them, and He shall wipe away every tear from their eyes; and there shall no longer be any death; there shall no longer be any mourning or crying, or pain; the first things have passed away . . . Behold, I am making all things new."*

This promise addresses past sorrows as well as future promises. In its simplest terms, these verses remind us that our suffering is temporary; the glory of God is eternal. One day God Himself—who will in our lifetime perfect, confirm, strengthen, and establish—will also fully heal and renew in glory. In heaven we will see and receive fully what Moses, Elijah, Peter, James, and John saw in a much-restricted manner. After John described heaven, as best he could, he informed us, "And there shall no longer be any curse; and the throne of God and of the Lamb shall be in it, and His bondservants shall serve Him; and they shall see His face, and His name shall be on their foreheads" (Rev. 22:3-4).

O come, Lord Jesus! All the promises of God exist in You. We look to You and long for You. We love You, but even more we acknowledge and marvel at the depths of Your great love for us. Come Thou Bright Morning Star. With the angelic host of heaven, we agree Thou alone are worthy to receive glory and honor and praise. Indeed, Thine is the kingdom . . . and the power . . . and especially the glory—forever and ever. Amen.

Also available from **Kress Christian**
PUBLICATIONS

The Cup and the Glory Study Guide
Greg Harris

One with a Shepherd: The Tears and Triumphs of a Ministry Marriage
Mary Somerville

Christian Living Beyond Belief: Biblical Principles for the Life of Faith
Cliff McManis

Meeting God Behind Enemy Lines: My Christian Testimony as a U.S. Navy SEAL
Steve Watkins

Revelation 20 and the Millennial Debate
Matt Waymeyer

Free Justification: The Glorification of Christ in the Justification of a Sinner
Steve Fernandez

God's Plan for Israel: A Study of Romans 9-11
Steve Kreloff

God in Everyday Life: The Book of Ruth for Expositors and Biblical Counselors
Brad Brandt & Eric Kress

Notes for the Study and Exposition of 1ˢᵗ John
Eric Kress

Commentaries for Biblical Expositors
Dr. Jim Rosscup

The Gromacki Expository Series (by Dr. Robert Gromacki)
Called to Be Saints: An Exposition of 1 Corinthians
Stand Firm in the Faith: An Exposition of 2 Corinthians
Stand Fast in Liberty: An Exposition of Galatians
Stand United in Joy: An Exposition of Philippians
Stand Perfect in Wisdom: An Exposition of Colossians & Philemon
Stand True to the Charge: An Exposition of 1 Timothy
Stand Bold in Grace: An Exposition of Hebrews

www.kresschristianpublications.com